THE MAP
TO NOWHERE

Chan Practice Guide
to Mind Cultivation

Chan Master
Chi Chern

Candlelight Books

The Map to Nowhere
—Chan Practice Guide to Mind Cultivation

This book is translated and edited from the Chinese work 繼程法師著《春在枝頭(二)》.

Printed in the United States of America

Library of Congress Cataloging-in-Publication Data

Chi Chern, 1955-

The Map to Nowhere – Chan Practice Guide to Mind Cultivation
ISBN 978-0-9970912-9-8 (paperback)

1. Chan (Zen) Meditation. 2. Chinese Buddhism.

I. Title: The Map to Nowhere – Chan Practice Guide to Mind Cultivation.
II. Chi Chern. III. Title.

Cover Art: Master Chi Chern
Calligraphy and Paintings: Master Chi Chern
Author Photography: Kongzhu Shi
Cover Design: Xing Chen
Editorial Assistant: Buffe Maggie Laffey

Candlelight Books
P. O. Box 7748
Berkeley, CA 94707

www.masterchichern.org

Contents

II. Teachings in Fourteen-day Advanced Retreat

自序

藏寶圖　藏啥寶
藏著自性清淨寶
清淨本性如來藏
因有雜染不顯露

尋寶圖　尋淨寶
圖文引導到寶藏
淨寶非是向外尋
如來本性心本性

如來藏　本性空
心行處滅言語斷
滅處心言語續
設計藏寶尋寶圖

藏寶圖　尋寶圖
皆是善巧方便度
見寶得寶一切空
當下當處即空靈

乙未十月十七
太平慈光寺

Preface

Master Chi Chern

The map of treasures…
What treasure? – The treasure of immaculate self.
Due to accumulated dust,
The treasure has been covered deep…

The map for treasure seekers,
Searching for the pure gem.
Guided by pictures and words, looking not out there
– Mind is the original nature.

Buddha-nature is originally empty,
Lying where mind ends and words stop.
From such a place words are used,
The map of treasure hunting is thus drawn.

Both treasure and the map,
Serve as expedient means to deliver beings.
When you see and attain true emptiness,
The treasure is nowhere but now here.

~ November 28, 2015, Taiping, Malaysia

Editor's Note

This is about an inward journey.

The destination is not out there.

What is being offered here is a map, which does not offer the kind of guidance that seasoned meditators might expect — it does not landmark various attractive locations nor charter the streets leading to the highly sought resorts. To serve these functions, there are already many manuals in the field on how to meditate or guidebooks for reaching samadhi or even enlightenment.

This book shares undecorated teachings in a relaxed chat-room, where sincere practitioners attend with their personal but commonly encountered obstacles during meditative practice, both on the cushion and in daily life.

You might be someone who has just begun to learn about meditation and participated in a few silent retreats; you might be someone who wonders why for years your diligence in meditation does not seem to make much difference or your practice has not yielded any breakthroughs — this book might be useful to you, directly!

Through the discourses given to participants in intensive retreats, and with his years of Chan practice and teaching experience, Chan Master Chi Chern offers intimate guidance on your journey to nowhere other than to the immaculate self as it originally is.

To the Buddhist population in the East, Chi Chern Fashi ("fashi," means Dharma master in Chinese) or Shifu as students in the East usually address him, is well known as a monk, teacher, and artist. It was not until 2008 that he began teaching in the West. Now Chan retreats led by Chi Chern Fashi are being offered in many countries and districts including Malaysia, Indonesia, Singapore, China, North America, Poland, England, Switzerland, Croatia, and Taiwan.

Chi Chern Fashi was born in Taiping, Malaysia, in 1955. He was ordained as a novice under the Very Venerable Zhu Mo (1913-2002) in Penang in 1978 and became a fully ordained bhikku the same year under Venerable

Masters Yin Shun, Yan Pei, and Zhen Hua in Taiwan. After graduating from the Chinese ddhism Research Institute of Fo Guang Shan in Taiwan in 1980, he learned Chinese Chan from Chan Master Sheng Yen (1930-2009) by participating in Master Sheng Yen's four consecutive retreats in Taipei, during which his profound experience of "seeing the true nature" was confirmed and Master Sheng Yen gave him permission to teach meditation. Between 1982 and 1984, Chi Chern Fashi undertook a thousand-day solitary retreat in Malaysia. In 1985, Master Sheng Yen formally bestowed on him Dharma Transmission with the name "Transmitting the Exoteric, Seeing the Esoteric" (Chuan Xian Jian Mi). This made him the first Dharma heir of Master Sheng Yen in the Linji lineage of Chinese Chan and a fourth generation Dharma descendent of Master Xu Yun (Empty Cloud).

In addition to teaching in formal Chan retreats, Chi Chern Fashi also teaches through his artwork in Chinese calligraphy, Chan paintings, poetry, Buddhist lyrics, and also tea. He refers to himself as the "Idle Monk from Taiping" (his birth place and residence) even though in addition to several other teaching and mentoring roles, he has also been the Principal of the Malaysian Buddhist Institute, Vice President of Malaysian Buddhist Association, and Abbot of Puzhao Buddhist Vihara. He said with great humility in one newspaper article, "I am not a Chan master." He lives a very simple and ordinary life indeed and is very approachable, almost instantly befriending anyone whom he meets — adults as well as children.

Why has this one book, among Chi Chern Fashi's over sixty published books, been chosen to be the first publication in English? This book includes discourses given in Malaysia in 1999 during two intensive retreats, prior to which all participants had learned the forms and basics of sitting meditation and had experienced intensive retreats. These discourses cover his essential teachings with detailed explanations concerning typical issues that many meditation practitioners encounter; they also cover instructions on how to deal with obstacles to practice, both in and out of the retreat environment. Therefore, this book serves as an excellent introductory of his Chan teachings to the practitioners in the West. It is best read as if one is attending a full seven-day Chan retreat and is having several individual consultation sessions with the teacher. Some of part I and part II cover similar topics since they are given in two separate retreats to different groups. Readers will find fresh approaches in each that the Master takes in order to meet the conditions and needs of various groups of participants.

To readers who are not yet familiar with Chinese Chan, particularly with the lineage of Master Sheng Yen, the frequently used word "method" throughout this book refers to the particular "method" or the "technique" which a practitioner finds helpful to practice in meditation, such as "counting breath," "asking the *huatou*," "reciting the name of the Buddha," etc. When the Master speaks about "returning to the method," it does not mean that there is "one" method that everyone employs in the retreat; instead, it is the particular method each participant practices currently. With this understanding, any method that assists in reaching stability and calmness of body and mind in order to achieve awareness and clarity is "the method" referred in the discourses.

The teachings in this book were given orally in the Chan hall and transcribed by students from audio recordings. After "direct" translations were completed in staying loyal to the original words of the Master, some editing was done with the intention of making the written presentation more compact or a bit clearer to audiences in the West. Although the translator has studied and lived in the United States for many years, the English rendered in this translation work is far from perfect. For this, the translator sincerely hopes that any barrier to the teachings caused by the translation or editing can be forgiven and overcome.

Among the many analogies employed in the teachings of Chi Chern Fashi, the "climbing the mountain" analogy vividly and best describes the complete journey of Chan practice or enlightenment. Whether you are on your way or have just arrived at the foot of the mountain, regardless of whether you are resting during the hike or heading towards the summit, the simple and clear, yet detailed and profound, teachings in these discourses offer guidance on establishing a solid foundation in Chan practice. As Chi Chern Fashi has pointed out, "nowhere" is "now here" — the present moment! So now, the rest of the journey is up to you!

Before concluding this brief introduction, as the translator and editor, I wish to thank a group of volunteers who have assisted in the completion

5

and publishing of this book — Nancy Townsend and Mary Gray for diligent assistance in English review and suggestions for editing; Buffe Laffey for lending her professional expertise in thorough editorial reviews; Xing Chen and De-Hua Zhang for assistance in cover designing; Yong Mo, Bo Feng, and Ting Ting Li for layout; Zhao-Qun He for matting work of all the artwork used in this book, and Paul Bridenbaugh for photo enhancement on the author image. I am very grateful to Reverend Kinrei Bassis and his congregation for their continued friendship and support — it was at their temple that I had focused time and quiet space to complete the majority of the work for this project. Also, many thanks go to Elan Wang and Yawen Hsu for their administrative assistance.

Words cannot sufficiently express my deep gratitude to Shifu — my teacher and mentor Master Chi Chern — for his profound yet down-to-earth teachings and his great compassion in guiding me through my study, practice, and global travel with him. This book is humbly dedicated to Shifu in the sixtieth year of his life on earth for celebrating his thirty-five years of Chan teaching around the world.

Kongzhu Shi
December 2015

I

Teachings in
Seven-day
Intensive Retreat

1

Facing Wandering Thoughts

In seated meditation, wandering thoughts are the first problem we typically encounter. Among the Five Hindrances to practice, (greed, anger, sloth, restlessness, and doubt), restlessness refers to these sorts of coarse, distractive and random thoughts. The continuity of these thoughts is not so easy to detect as they drift around. However, when we do pay attention in daily life, we notice restlessness in the mind as we face the karmic consequences of our unwholesome speech and actions. Due to the interference of wandering thoughts, particularly in the beginning stage, practitioners feel unable to use meditation methods effectively.

A Closer Look at Wandering Thoughts

During sitting meditation, there seems to always be a force trying to pull our attention away, making it difficult to concentrate. External objects in the environment distract us. Internally, our complex and chaotic thoughts drive our attention all over the place.

When the method cannot be adopted successfully in practice, we usually feel restless. If, in addition, the environment is not ideal for meditation — for example, the light is too bright or there is too much noise — we are more likely to feel restless. In seated meditation, the sense faculty of the eyes usually withdraws from external distractions; but if the light is too strong, this ability will be impacted. Also, as eyesight is becoming isolated from outward objective conditions, the sense faculty of the ears becomes more sensitive. In this circumstance, mental quietude can be easily disturbed by sound. If the body is not well adjusted and relaxed, and there is leg pain or back ache, it is not easy to implement the method effectively. This is what happens most often to the majority of participants in the beginning few days of a seven-day or ten-day Chan retreat.

However, if you have consistently practiced with the method in your daily routine — such as having a fixed time for sitting, training yourself to inwardly collect and concentrate, studying the Dharma to make your life in accord with the Buddha's teachings, and making adjustments to harmonize the mind and body in daily life — in intensive retreat, the disturbance of unfavorable outward conditions will tend to diminish and restlessness will take place less frequently or with less intensity. You might notice the continuous movement of wandering thoughts, but the condition of the mind is different from the beginning when you were unable to adopt the method.

On the other hand, if you seldom sit and meditate, or if it has been a long while since you did meditative practice, when you enter the Chan hall in retreat, you will be unable to settle easily. Restlessness will show up more readily and more obviously. You will find wandering thoughts constantly pulling your attention away, or you will feel a lack of strength and your brain will not comply with your wishes. Unable to apply the method, many wandering thoughts will arise, some of which will make you want to hurry and force the use of the method. Unfortunately, the more anxious you are, the coarser the wandering thoughts will be. Having all kinds of disturbances, it will be even more challenging to employ the method. Therefore, it is very important to train the body and cultivate the mind in daily life.

When you are able to focus and observe your thoughts a little bit, you will discover that wandering thoughts are reflections of your daily life. As you observe more carefully, you will see that these thoughts also reflect your personality and various internal conditions. The impact of your activities in daily life comes to the surface with these thoughts. You will know yourself better because what is reflected in the wandering thoughts is intimately related to you. In other words, these thoughts are the karmic consequences of your actions.

What usually appears in the mind is a manifestation of what is identified in Buddhism as the "Twelve-Linked Chain of Causes and Conditions". They are categorized as ignorance, karma (actions and consequences) and suffering. Many things in daily life are displeasing to us and we react with afflictions. If our wandering thoughts correspond with anger, thoughts of aversion arise. If wandering thoughts are in line with greed and thoughts of liking pop up, awareness is quickly grabbed by it. When wandering thoughts are chaotic, this is suffering; when one cannot successfully apply the method in seated meditation, this is also suffering. When such occurrences take place, combined with restlessness, suffering turns into confusion and ignorance in both intellect and emotion. With troubled thoughts arising, annoyances are stirred up and further drive one to feel more mental pain or torment.

Hence, when one cannot actually use the method in meditation, it often turns the mental condition into a vicious cycle. One becomes more anxious and the wandering thoughts push annoyances around in a more abrasive fashion. It continues on and on and forms a chain that is endless — a cycle of ignorance, karmic deeds and consequences, and inescapable suffering.

Essential Approach to Settle the Mind

When wandering thoughts arise, it is useful to take the approach of "calming" to help halt the cycle. Although the method of "calming" itself does not end suffering, at least it slows down the running stream of wandering thoughts and in some cases may bring it to a stop.

The practice of "calming" is returning to the method of meditation no matter what happens and regardless of how coarse the thoughts. As soon as wandering thoughts are detected or unease is sensed, immediately pulling the attention back and staying focused on the method helps to prevent suffering from becoming ignorance and karma-bearing actions. Allowing suffering to continue to develop will result in confusion and ignorance, which will intensify the movement of wandering thoughts. Therefore, make an effort to pull the attention back to the method — the method will assist in keeping focus.

Under such conditions, the suffering will lose its strength and momentum. Even though wandering thoughts may still pass through, the mind can remain undisturbed.

The first thing to do in this approach is to concentrate, letting the awareness focus on one object. This one object is needed in order to collect the thoughts. Counting the breaths, for example, will help stop the attention from being scattered. You can settle the awareness on the breath first, and then count the breaths to stay focused.

At the beginning stage of practice, the method of "counting the breaths" can help with waking up the function of awareness. If you begin with the method of "following the breath" instead of counting, without your knowing it the attention can easily be pulled away by wandering thoughts or by what happens in the environment. Until attention is brought back to the breath, you might be fooling yourself by thinking that your practice with the method was uninterrupted while, in actuality, awareness was already lost in the operation and the method was "abandoned". This is the reason it is recommended to use "breath counting" as an aid, for when you lose the count, you will know you have drifted away and awareness has been dropped. It alerts you that you were not with the method during that stretch of time. It reminds you to gather your strength and pull your attention back again to the method. If you merely pay attention to the breath and do not count your breaths, when you lose awareness, you will not even notice. Therefore, at the beginning of employing a method, it is helpful to use "breath counting" to settle your mind.

Since at the beginning of practice wandering thoughts are coarse, we adopt a relatively coarse method — counting the breath — to counteract. Usually the condition in our mind is not cultivated and refined. Not only is our awareness often lost, but also our ability to focus is nowhere to be found. Yet we may naively think that we are conducting the practice with diligence. This is similar to the situation where we think we do not have wild thoughts until we sit and meditate. Only then do we find many wandering thoughts racing in our head. The wandering thoughts were actually much more complex and chaotic before we took up the practice, we were just not aware of them. As the five sense faculties are drawn outward day in and day out, when did we find time to reflect within? Only when we sit and meditate — because the attention is focused and our awareness is awakened — do we discover so many wandering thoughts that were hidden. Focusing on an object allows us to be aware of what we are doing; only then do we see the conditions in our mind. Therefore, to the majority of practitioners, counting the breaths is a very useful, seemingly basic, but absolutely essential method with which to begin.

When you do really well in breath counting, the abilities of concentration and awareness will come into sync. Then you can discontinue counting and just focus on the breath. Only then will you be truly "following" the breath. If you feel that following the breath is the only way you can manage at the beginning and are unable to do the counting, this is an indication that you are not using the method, or using it improperly to say the least. In this case, what you are doing is still in the scope of regulating the breath. The breathing of those who can actually "follow" the breath is very subtle and refined. If needed, these practitioners can count the breaths without any problem. If practice is more refined, going back to a method that is relatively coarse does not pose an issue. It would be fine if, after counting the breaths for a few moments, they feel counting is too coarse and then choose to drop the counting.

There can be times when you follow the breath but after two minutes your attention becomes scattered, perhaps for five minutes. You come back to counting again for another two minutes, not knowing that during the five minutes in between, you had lost awareness and were not with your method. You linked the two minutes before and after, thinking that you were practicing diligently. With the assistance of counting, however, when you lose your count, it will immediately reveal that you were not with the method and, for five minutes, your awareness was absent. As you may have already experienced, when awareness is not present, it is not difficult at all to become a wanderer. Hence, counting the breath can help monitor for us whether we are practicing the method or not.

Returning to the Method

The purpose of using a method, such as mindfulness of the breath, is to bring the attention to settle and the mind to be at ease. During seated meditation, if you find that there are many wandering thoughts dragging you all over the place, try the best you can to bring your attention back to the method. Do not allow the thoughts to form a churning pattern, for you are likely to feel agitated when you are unable to count the breaths without interruptions or when your legs are in screaming pain. When agitation turns into annoyance, it produces more wandering thoughts that make you feel more irritated. The whole cyclic process can escalate very rapidly. From the time you feel leg pain or are interrupted by what happens in your surroundings, to the time of failing to apply the method, many wandering thoughts flood through. It can turn out that, after a period of sitting, all you have is agitation and more agitation. As you suffer this sort of impediment, wandering thoughts become increasingly coarse and turbulent, and even when it is time to exit from meditation, you can still be agitated. Therefore, when you are unable to adopt the method and wandering thoughts are coarse, do not fight against them. Gradually but surely, with your continued diligence in practice, they will subside and eventually stop being disturbances.

Knowing this is the case, no matter what situation occurs, try everything you can to bring the awareness back to the method. Use the method to help minimize the recycling of wandering thoughts. The entire process is like a battle with a seesaw — when the attention is pulled away, you must try firmly pulling it back. Otherwise, it will run wild, out of control. Even if you are able to bring the focus back, remember that there will still be residual energy urging you to go outward. This is because the long-accumulated habitual wandering thoughts are more stubborn than we can imagine.

It is usually the case in daily life that people spend more time with wandering thoughts than with awareness, isn't it? If one sits in meditation less than half an hour or an hour a day and less than two or three days a week, imagine how much time one spends on having wandering thoughts and how much time on awareness! We can understand, then, why wandering thoughts are so strong. Of course not all wandering thoughts are unwholesome. However, when wholesome thoughts and deluded thoughts are jumbled together, we find the strength of mindfulness is rather weak. Nonetheless, when practicing with a method, even though there are endless wandering thoughts constantly flowing through, try to bring the attention back to the method and use one object to focus your attention. The power of the flowing force of wandering thoughts will undoubtedly be diminished.

When your practice has reached a phase where the attention can gradually focus on the method, it is not abnormal to notice that there are still flows of wandering thoughts. But now you can ignore them and simply focus on the method, allowing wandering thoughts to arise and pass. When the attention is able to settle down and the use of the method has become fairly stable, the attention is not so easily distracted even as wandering thoughts arise. At such times, you can use this stabilized state of mind to observe the wandering thoughts.

If you cannot settle down with ease, the ability to focus will not be sharp. Then you will not have sufficient strength to penetrate the nature of all phenomena in contemplation even though in daily life you can function normally with thoughts moving about. You must try to train yourself to reach relative quietude. In a tranquil state, focusing awareness on one object for a period of time will yield strength. Then you can employ this strength to go deep and cultivate liberating insight.

Conditions of Our Mind

Very often, the condition in our mind is untamed and not under our control. When wandering thoughts run around, we are like a monkey, readily distracted. Even though sometimes we are capable of planning and organizing, this governing ability is usually entangled in afflictions. No wonder things often do not work as we originally planned or expected! When afflictions become overwhelming, our thinking becomes the victim of our vexations. Such conditions in the mind are revealed to us when we do try to organize our thoughts.

Some people's mind conditions are more trained or refined, and their actions are more carefully thought through. But when facing obstacles or adverse circumstances, can their mind conditions remain refined? Will their reactions be calm and clear when they are unpleasantly stimulated? Actually what we think ought to be done often results in conflicting situations. For example, when you are sitting in meditation, initially you intend to reflect on the Buddhadharma; but after a while, somehow it becomes another situation — you find that it is no longer the Dharma but a pile of afflictions that are occupying your mind. Furthermore, as soon as you act upon them, unwholesome karma has already been created.

Usually if we are not thinking about the past, we are thinking about the future. We never seem to settle in the present. Sometimes we sit and think about life, or construct some goals that we want to achieve. At some point, if we are aware, we will find that what we wished to accomplish is no longer within the scope of the original design but slowly has turned into another thing! From this we can tell that often we are not in charge and the power of wandering thoughts is well beyond our imagination. We did not notice this condition until we practiced meditation.

When the streams of wandering thoughts arrive, it is like ocean waves, one after another, rushing up relentlessly. When we start to entertain one thought, we think, think, and think, until at one point we stop. But if we put the first thought and the last thought of the process together and compare them, we find that what they are concerned about are quite far apart from each other, if not completely alien. As the Chinese idiom says, "Wind and horses or ox are not even nearly relatives." We are unable to recall how they followed one another since it all went too quickly. This is what we might notice in the mind at the beginning stage of our practice.

Usually, the time we are mindful is rather sparse. The majority of the time we are following wandering thoughts. Although occasionally mindful thoughts arise, often they are mixed with wandering thoughts. For instance, someone practices reciting the name of the Buddha. Even though they are doing it sincerely, the name of the Buddha is blended with wandering thoughts and the Buddha's name is only one of the many thoughts. This is why such recitation practice lacks the desired impact even though some people feel it is fairly effective if they can practice diligently like this.

Examine carefully for yourself the conditions under which you usually practice mindfulness of the Buddha. Is it the wandering or scattered thought that is reciting the name of the Buddha? With scattered thoughts reciting or merely mouthing some syllables, there is no awareness. Occasionally the name of the Buddha may float up, and if it happens that you notice it, you might think that you are practicing with diligence, while actually it has no significance, much less any spiritual power. As soon as a strong thought or external object arises, who knows where the name of the Buddha went! After a while, as a habit, the Buddha's name floats out again, and awareness returns for a brief moment. This is what happens most of the time when people try to practice mindfulness.

The uncultivated condition of our mind is a mixture of wholesome and unwholesome thoughts. As thoughts flow around, how much mental power do we have to maintain conscious thinking? If conscious thinking is strong, it will be easier to be aware and keep the thoughts in accord with the Buddhadharma. If there are countless wandering thoughts around while intended thoughts appear only occasionally, then there is not much strength in the mind. Hence we should try our best to settle on the method. As our focus and awareness become stronger, the strength of willpower will gradually increase. Then we will be able to cast off the wandering thoughts that are in the unwholesome camp. The method we use, regardless of whether it is from the standpoint of "calming" or "contemplating insight", is to first gain some strength of concentration. Then it will have some commanding power in practice.

If we are able to continuously keep mindful thoughts when we do contemplation, we can better respond to the world and make choices with right mindfulness. Every moment in life we are faced with all kinds of situations that require responding, including when we are asleep. In sleep, although the five sense faculties are not in reaction mode, consciousness is still functioning. While we are awake, the five sense faculties come in and out non-stop to transport information. Upon receiving the information, with what thoughts do we respond? Chan practice is to raise or sharpen our awareness. If, in perceiving the nature of all phenomena through contemplation, our awareness is in harmony with the Buddhadharma, and we maintain right mindfulness, our response will be in accord with Buddhadharma.

It would be genuine enlightenment if we realized the true nature of all dharma or phenomena. However, before reaching this point, we need to at least maintain the practice of letting right mindful thinking occupy the mind, and deal with what we encounter in daily life with awareness or clarity. If we can do so, we will realize that our responses are different than what they would have been with a mind full of wandering thoughts and afflictions. It will save a great deal of trouble if we can act according to the Buddhadharma and stop creating all sorts of problems for ourselves and for others.

When we react based on afflictions, various kinds of unease are generated. For example, you dislike somebody who might have given you a hard time in the past. You want to retaliate now and you think it will make you happy. But afterward, you begin to feel unease, worrying about whether sometime he or she will suddenly shoot an arrow and hurt you again.

From coarse to subtle, there is a condition of vexations in our mind that can be perturbed by stimulants. As soon as this condition starts to operate, it generates a feeling of fear or unease. Too often what we do in daily life creates recurrences of such mental conditions. Its impact is so pervasive that, once done, it will repeat itself. However, when you come across your "enemy", if you employ right thought, recognizing that everyone makes mistakes and that before becoming a saint even a noble person can make mistakes, you can then tolerate and forgive that person. In this case, you will no longer be burdened with fear or worry. Since the cultivation of mind has not yet reached such a level, it is not entirely effortless to accept the perceived enemy. Once we consider others as enemies, we desire to resist them. This is common to most people. However, if we can treat what happens with the Buddhadharma, knowing that all phenomena are empty and devoid of self-existing substance, we can be harmonious with others without discrimination — for then who is the enemy? Why would one need to think of retaliation? Fear and worry will be gone. If we can see things with compassion and wisdom, all problems cease to exist, and the cycle of samsara or suffering ends.

Unfortunately, in day-to-day life, we manufacture vicious cycles all the time. When we are in contact with the outside world, our decisions are often influenced by our habitual energy. As we grow older, the condition of our mind becomes more complex. Our life is full of variety. We create lots of things and hold on to them non-stop, as if once possessed, they can be depended upon and will make us feel safe. We become utterly afraid of losing them. In order to have the sense of security, we create another set of conditions that are the same. For example, some women believe that they must be in relationship with a man, and that if they have a man, they will be secure in life. But after capturing one, they are afraid of losing him. Every day they feel anxious because of him. Before they had a boyfriend, life seemed to be empty. After they are in the relationship, is life really meaningful and safe? Do they feel they have finally achieved security? Nowadays, many women have their own job and can be independent and do not need to rely on men to survive. But does life have a real sense of security? It does not seem to be so. You see, we are creating problems for ourselves every day. When will our mind be truly at peace?

Another example is when we take vacations. Does vacation make us really relaxed or more tired? In the old days, a mother is on vacation when the children are on vacation. But nowadays, when the kids are on school breaks, the mother is busier because the children have extra assignments to study during the holidays. When I was attending school, a break was a break — there was no need to get up early in the morning and our mother did not need to get up early to prepare breakfast for us. Now it is quite different. Even though there is no class at seven o'clock, there is a tutoring session perhaps at seven thirty in the morning — the same, if not busier, schedule! It seems that there is no moment that we can really relax.

Practice In Retreat

Participating in a Chan retreat ought to be really relaxing. We simply go to meals at mealtime. When the bell rings, we go to the Chan hall for sitting meditation. Although we must get up at three or four o'clock in the morning, with such a routine, we can put aside many of our worldly concerns. Even if we may not resolve our afflictions during the retreat, at least we do not have to think about them for the time being. To a certain degree, such a life is almost like an escape. Sometimes it is helpful, for we can avoid lots of complexity and return to simplicity.

Many times we feel powerless and that we are not the masters of our life. Even our own thought does not listen to our commands! Our attention moves with external situations, chasing after this or that, running around constantly and becoming more and more complex. Now that we are practicing with determination during the retreat, can we change our old habits? The fact is, before we can truly stop the cycles of ignorance, we will continue to flow and fluctuate with the streams of samsara.

If you begin to truly understand and diminish the complicity of the mundane, the forces of the cyclic dynamics will be lessened. When you have a wandering thought, you can drop it temporarily, and return to the method. Then you will find that unnecessary stuff you had believed you "cannot live without" has been slowly released because now you have discovered its insignificance, and you are simply fine without it. Many things are like this. Once clinging to something, you feel you cannot live without it. For instance, some young fellows, when their lovers left them, felt as though everything had collapsed and it was the end of the whole universe. It is the same story in other areas of life.

Hence, when you are determined to do the practice, no matter how strong the restlessness you feel, or how powerfully the wandering thoughts flood in your mind, regardless of what happens, try your utmost to return to the method. You can use the method of counting the breaths to slow down the moving force of wandering thoughts. If you cannot even do this, there is no simpler method for you to utilize. The simple approach of returning to the method is actually very powerful. If you are able to grasp the essence of it and practice well, you can then see how to further deal with other problems you encounter in meditation.

Should you feel there is nothing you need to fathom, then simply sit with the method. You will likely make some significant progress in your practice, and the condition in the mind will be more refined through the process. When your awareness is truly with the method, its strength will be enhanced enormously.

If you are unable to practice with any method at this time, do not worry. You can take a look and reflect on the life you have lived in the past. You may find that many decisions you made previously were unproductive or unsupportive of meditative practice, and perhaps you wish to make adjustments. You can utilize the time during the retreat to keep a distance from your hectic life and allow yourself some mental space to really let go of the trivia of daily life in order to bring harmony to mind and body. Later when you look back, you will feel fresh and different, and you can see things with more clarity.

2

Dealing with Wandering Thoughts

In practice we experience lots of wandering thoughts in the mind. There are at least two approaches to handle this. One is to ignore them, keep coming back to the method and let the wandering thoughts pass, one stream after another. Another is by relaxing. Because we encounter a myriad of things in everyday life, our body feels tired and the mind scattered when we sit and meditate in the evening, and it is very difficult to apply the method. At such times, as long as the sitting posture is upright, you can just relax the body and let the wandering thoughts settle without intentional engagement. This approach can facilitate the diminishment of those wandering thoughts that are on the surface, discouraging them from sticking to the mind.

Simple Awareness

Wandering thoughts are often accumulated in the mind. This is because we do not sort them out properly in a timely manner. Normally wandering thoughts would not be deeply imbedded in the mind. However, if they are not dealt with today, they are carried on to the next day. New things are added on and press this layer of wandering thoughts inward to the back of the mind. Each day, as we continuously collect these wandering or deluded thoughts, the mind quietly tolerates them. When a layer is added, if the "stuff" is something we had experienced before, the impression in the mind becomes deeper. If what happened today is unfamiliar or not the same as experienced in the past, then what happened not long ago would be pushed even further back since we have now added a new layer of stuff. Over time these unprocessed wandering thoughts become more complex and eventually become very muddled.

However, if we deal with these wandering thoughts in timely manner — for instance each day — they will not accumulate layer upon layer. But we are unable to sort out all wandering thoughts since some of them are buried rather deeply in our mind. When the five sense faculties come into contact with the outside world and information flows in, hidden memories of past experiences are stirred up. This causes emotional reactions in us and we are unable to clear them up immediately.

Some people say that things of the past are forgotten. Actually, many things which happened yesterday are already forgotten, not to mention things in the remote past. While not everything in the world that we are in contact with, nor every single situation in daily life, cause us to have a reaction that penetrates deeply through our mind, a portion of them do recycle for a long time and become our habits. Take a body movement as an example. At the beginning we are unaware of it. After we have done it for some time, it becomes a habitual move or gesture of personal style. Our habits and afflictions are all accumulated bit by bit over time. However, if handled in a timely manner, unwanted behavior will not stay with us for too long.

If you are able to practice diligently every day, you can simply concentrate on the method and let the wandering thoughts come and go. If you are unable to stay with the method or have lack of strength to focus, you should relax the body. Do not use deliberate thinking or try to make anything happen. Simply let the mind sink like dust settling in a lake. This can help eliminate some wandering thoughts. Should your ability to focus become fairly stable, you may then try resolving some issues that are deep. Otherwise, what you deal with will just be on the surface. What is important is to avoid driving them deeper inward and getting their energy more accumulated over time.

Sometimes when you sit down, something arises and stirs your emotion. If you go with it, it will recycle itself. For instance, let's say that you just had an argument with someone before sitting. It stirred your anger and the angry emotion gets repeated one more time. Not only is the anger repeated, but also you add something to it by remembering some critical words you forgot to say during the argument and imagining that, with these words, you might have beaten that person. People often tend to spin this type of karma.

To deal with wandering thoughts, try doing nothing but letting the wandering thoughts arise and cease by themselves. If you have a thought about cleaning up the wandering thoughts, this thought itself is also a wandering thought. For example, when you sit, some wandering thoughts show up and you feel restless. Restlessness is similar to anger. Can you use one angry thought to clear up other angry thoughts? Because you do not like those thoughts, you attempt to use one thought to chase out the other thoughts. But this thought might be coarser than the other thoughts. The disturbance it causes may be more violent. In the end, instead of being chased away, their presence continues and intensifies.

Thoughts are psychological elements. They are composed to emerge as thoughts, which are nothing but phenomena. The sense faculty of consciousness is discriminative and incapable of pushing these phenomena away, just like when we open our eyes we cannot help but see objects, our ears hear sounds, and our nose smells odors. How do you drive off smell? How do you chase away sounds? It is impossible to dispel any phenomenon confronting us. Wanting to chase phenomena away indicates that there is dislike in the mind. For instance, you do not like it when you hear noise. You may have various kinds of reactions but these are to no avail. This is why when you sit and meditate, and as wandering thoughts arise, you should not use anger to battle with them. If you do that, it only fuels the anger and recycles it one more time. The anger becomes stronger and will return very soon. Trying to drive off thoughts will aggravate them even more. All karma is created like this, not only in thoughts but also in consciousness.

Pleasant experiences tend to offer us long-lasting impressions; unpleasant things also easily leave deep impressions in our mind. Because of the likes and dislikes, we give wandering thoughts the permission to repeat. Therefore, knowing that we cannot chase them away, the only alternative is to let them arise and cease by themselves. Let them go as they pass — do not engage with them. Usually this technique can reduce many thoughts in daily life that are not charged with so much invested energy — karma of lesser intensity. When you sit down and relax the body, let those thoughts arise and pass. If they do not resonate with inner conflict or past experiences in the consciousness, they will be forgotten very quickly.

Much of what happens every day is forgotten. However, what is forgotten may not have passed. Sometimes this function of forgetting is somewhat healing. We choose to forget because our mind needs healing or to regain a certain level of balance. In some cases, we have to lock up some unpleasant experiences, temporarily forgetting them; otherwise our conditon becomes unbearable. If we let them fade for a while and the mind has gained strength, when they come up again we may have the energy to face and handle them. In psychotherapy sessions, a psychotherapist may note that a patient has certain habitual body movements and may ask the person to recall their past. Actually all of the past is in the mental repository of the patient; the patient just may not want to remember it. Frequently when someone wants to comfort us in times of difficulty, they like to chat with us about something in the past. However, sometimes we do not wish to speak about it because it brings sensations of hurt or depression. So we take the medicine of forgetting in order to cover it up. This does not actually solve the problem for us but to a certain degree, it does save us from completely disastrous collapse. If we let all of them suddenly explode, sometimes the consequences can be quite serious. So we forget them temporarily in order to lessen their impact. As those unimportant or less disturbing experiences pass, eventually they will be completely over and ended.

In seated meditation, if your body is too tired and you feel too mentally scattered, the method you are trying to practice will not work as expected. Under these circumstances, the way to efficiently respond is to simply relax the body and mind. If you are able to practice well with your method, then by all means, try to stay with the method. Use the method to collect yourself and let the wandering thoughts pass, stream after stream, strengthening the willpower for more proactive actions. When you feel settled, your willpower strong, and your ability to contemplate stable, then you can take the step of observing your wandering thoughts. Being inwardly collected, with sharp concentration and awareness, you can see the wandering thoughts clearly. Only then will you be someone who has departed from the complex and confused thought stream.

Breaking Habits

Chan practice actually is a method of breaking habits. Our habits move according to our thoughts. Now we are trying to let the mind stay in a quiet and stable condition, allowing our attention to withdraw from the stream of wandering thoughts. It is like when we are in a crowd of people. If we follow the crowd, we cannot see the situation with clarity; but if we step out, we can observe clearly what is really going on. If you feel your awareness is not stable enough yet, then let the flow of wandering thoughts go, but you yourself do not move with it. When you feel more grounded and resilient, you can watch the circus of wandering thoughts.

As we observe wandering thoughts, we will see that they actually reflect our life, our personality, and our deep-rooted afflictions. Almost everything can be revealed in the activities of wandering thoughts. If we see them clearly, we can be perceptive and at some stage of practice, wisdom will gradually but steadily develop. We will find that we have learned a lot about ourselves, society at large, and about all human beings on earth — all at the same time.

When we see our wandering thoughts and emotions of anger or greed come up, we will understand the issue of pollution on earth and the fact that we are part of it. Do not think, "We are environmentalists, so we can purify the earth." In fact, if we cannot transform our own thoughts and purify the conditions of our own mind, it is impossible to cleanse the earth and establish a Pure Land on this planet. If you believe that it is other people who pollute the earth but not you, and you strategize against those people, you are adding violence by your disapproval or protests. This is no different from walking with those who cause damage, only that they are farther ahead — maybe they walked a hundred steps and you did fifty — but both are contributing to the devastating problems on earth. With practice, you realize that if you do not clean up your own mess but only hope to purify others, the task of cleaning the environment is utterly impossible to accomplish. We know that water can be used to clean things, but if the water is dirty, can it be used for cleaning? Maybe it can be used for washing something off, but the result is questionable.

When you do the practice of observation and contemplation, the mind must be still and have unwavering strength. Otherwise, wandering thoughts will spoil it. If your practice lacks strength of mind, you will find that many times you try to observe wandering thoughts but in the end, the "seeing" itself also becomes a wandering thought and runs off with these other wandering thoughts. It is as if you stand at a crossroad watching streams of people, some of whom you have interest in and whom you step out to follow. Originally you were just standing there and watching — now you have joined them, and people who stand on the street will be watching you!

From these phenomena we know that we have a great deal of training to do, for we are incredibly quick in losing awareness. Do not deceive yourself by imagining that your mind is purified and liberated when you are observing impurity on the cushion. In reality, if you are unable to clearly see through the wandering thoughts, how can you handle your multitude of problems? There will be no way for you to begin cleansing them.

Sometimes we want to substitute wandering thoughts with mindfulness. We may wish there would be a way to clear up all the wandering thoughts or completely replace them with mindfulness, and we hope that there is a magic technique for that. But honestly speaking, only when we are in seated meditation may we have a glimpse of right mindfulness; at other times, right mindfulness tells us to progress towards wholesomeness while deluded thoughts urge us, "don't bother, follow me." We are kind of seesawing in between — one side encourages us to swim against the stream and let the power of wandering thoughts subside, while the other wants us to wander along and not settle down. The former is mindfulness and the latter is unwholesome or deluded thoughts. The wandering thoughts are a mixture of all of these. To see through our thoughts clearly, we must strive to strengthen the power of self-discipline in the mind and the function of awareness.

Discipline with Simplicity

When we observe our wandering thoughts with clarity, we can be shocked to discover that, all along, the simple mind we believed we had is filled with so many complex thoughts. We usually think we are very simple but, in actuality, the mind of a human being is incredibly complex. There is a tendency for people to make things or life complicated. Something very simple can make everybody involved incredibly busy and unhappy — as if that would be fun! Many people like to add things to something simple by guessing another's mind with their own tricky thoughts. Why? It is habitual — they are accustomed to doing it since the habitual energy is so irresistible.

Someone often advises others by saying, "Turn the big matter into small, and turn small things to nothing". Actually the world itself has no problem, but somebody insists on making something out of nothing as if only then would life be rich and have some meaning. The so-called rich or meaningful is just chasing external conditions and many people are happy to do that. Some people take pleasure in others' misfortune. If we honestly look at our mind, we can find demonic thoughts at times. Are we really as virtuous as we thought we were? When we examine our thoughts thoroughly, we may be stunned, "My goodness, I am such a bad person!" Of course it is not true that people are really evil. It is just that sometimes deluded thoughts are indeed present. Because we absorb a tremendous amount of information in the world, we are influenced to think in a similar way, whether intentional or not.

Out of habit, we may think excessively about something that is very simple, often guessing with our own little psyche what others might think, or guarding ourselves tightly against this or that. Consequently, when we interact with people, we are like what the proverb says, "Only speak one third of what need to be said to other people" — as if the end of the world would come if we revealed our mind one hundred percent naked! This is all because our thoughts are too complex. We do too much scheming, and therefore all kinds of trouble manifest. If we can analyze further as these tricky thoughts appear, we find that we really suffer in the mind, and it is a serious disease. Yet, we treat it as if it is a smart trait, mistaking suffering as joy.

Each day we use many external things to fill the mind, so when we sit and meditate, we feel uneasy and desperately want to fill it with something familiar. When wandering thoughts arise, as if it was not burdensome enough, we fill the mind with bundles of concepts, opinions, plus everything else thoughts can produce. When the mind is over packed without any space, we finally realize that we have problems! Try and visualize this — A room is full of people; if another person wants to squeeze in, the people in the room would complain. When someone inside pushes and wants to get out, the crowd also complains. If someone attempts to do something in order to expand the capacity of the room, all people involved would have to bear the disruption and experience this sort of "pain in the neck." If we really take the time to observe our mind in depth, is suffering truly something external? No. It is all manufactured by our thinking.

To wish for peace of the world, first our mind must be peaceful. When our mind is truly peaceful, we will find peace in the world. If there is no peace in our mind, it is impossible to achieve world peace because in the process of obtaining world peace, we may have planted seeds of new problems. The peace we are now pursuing is merely some balance of phenomena. We consider the apparent balance more important than true equanimity, so we pursue superficial balance; but it is accomplished only temporarily. This is why we find that, after maintaining balance for a while, wars between groups or countries break out again, because the balance is man-made with unnatural forces. We do the same with our mind — Instead of subtracting when imbalance is recognized, we add something in an attempt to bring balance. If the addition is excessive and the scale skews towards one end, we hurry to add something more on the other end. How much can the mind be burdened with such repeated acts? We add internally when there is imbalance in the external; and we add something externally when there is imbalance in the internal. Such attempts may gain some measure of balance but, still, it is relative in the macroscope. The net outcome is that there is always fluctuation up and down in our mind, and problems are continuously generated.

The practice of Chan is to make effort in bringing the thoughts to settle and to have power of self-discipline and mastery. During sitting meditation, continuing to return to the method is, in a way, subtracting from the over-burdened mind. This is because we do not cling to the wandering thoughts, nor do we manipulate the flow or get pulled away by them — we only focus our attention on the method. This is the reason why the method for practice must be simple, for then we can quietly settle our mind in a reasonable amount of time.

We need to strengthen the power of self-mastery, which is challenging.

If the power of insight is not strong, wandering thoughts easily pull our attention away. Therefore we must increase our capacity of observation, perceive everything clearly, learn about it, and comprehend it thoroughly. According to the Buddhadharma, what is right mindfulness? What are deluded or unwholesome thoughts? We can look within and see which category of thoughts is overwhelmingly occupying the mental space. If we suffer in the mind, it is an indication that deluded thoughts are running wild and we should clean the mess. The method for cleansing is to watch or illuminate with bright awareness.

We are afraid or hesitant to watch our thoughts when we feel a lack of mental strength so we just focus on the method and let the thoughts pass. As we gain inner strength, we can start to examine the thoughts and see clearly both wholesome and unwholesome thoughts. Usually they are mixed together. Try your best to keep an objective observation, not letting yourself be pulled away but allowing the wandering thoughts to drop off layer after layer. As you firmly apply the method, slowly the coarse thoughts will subside — at least for a while before another stream of thoughts arrives.

Self-Awakening

Wandering thoughts are not all in the same category. They have patterns and different degrees of depth or intensity. The more refined mind is able to notice more subtle thoughts, which are somewhat different from the chaotic and complex thoughts that are experienced at the beginning of practice.

At the beginning of practice, we are constantly distracted by coarse wandering thoughts, and so we experiences restlessness in the mind. However, what we often face is not something taking place in the moment but images of past experiences. This type of wandering thought is subtle, organized, and not very strong. These thoughts can reveal issues deep in our psyche, such as why we have certain habits. After careful examination and reflection, we can see that the behavior at a particular time was caused by some subtle afflictions. If we put wandering thoughts into groups, subtle afflictions can be easily categorized but coarse ones may not be that easy.

We know all vexations are in the category of greed, anger, or ignorance, but there are different types of vexations. For example, in the category of greed, we know that everyone has desires — some people are obsessed with sex; some have craving for scent, sound or sensual touch, etc. — but not everyone has the same taste. What one person likes, another person may dislike. For instance, sometimes men cannot tolerate accompanying women shopping because what women like is not typically what men would be crazy about. Of course, this is not universally true and should not be generalized. In some cases, perhaps we feel something is not a big deal, but someone else may deem it outrageous. We might treat something as a piece of cake, but to others, it might be horrendous. On the other hand, something we treat very critically, others might consider ridiculous and wonder how we can be angry with such pitiful little matters! As we calm down and see the wandering thoughts with clarity, many layers of them can be put into categories.

If we take a good look into the deep-rooted afflictions, we find that we are part of the problems we cause. We often criticize society or others, but at such times, we should really reflect on ourselves. Perhaps if we know we are actually the one who is "useless", we will be willing to admit that it is useless to blame others. All the mistakes we condemn in others can be found in ourselves. They are all hidden in our thoughts. This is the reason why we see them out there in others. Those who have a tendency to be jealous very often sense it in others since the vibration is the same, and so they are rather sensitive and tune into it.

We all want to change others, but do we ever want to change ourselves? There is absolutely no need to criticize others because we are one of them. It is better that we adjust ourselves and manage our own thoughts well. In the process of doing so, we spread positive energy to society and help people awaken. True enlightenment begins with awakening of the self. If this self-awakening comes after our body is born, we need enlightened beings to awaken us. After we have awakened, we can then illuminate the path for others. Those who are awakened after birth were enlightened by awakened beings. They learned from the enlightened ones and were willing to change and improve themselves. In such a process, they help others to wake up, and thus, in totality, the society can be transformed.

Sometimes we feel depressed seeing that wandering thoughts are negative and countless, and we think, "Gosh, how can I be such a terrible person?" and we feel hopeless about ourselves. We may have this sort of emotion when we have difficulty in applying the method in our practice. On one hand, we are unable to generate the energy to practice with diligence; on the other, we are impatient in wanting to change the outward and inward conditions. Both are not the correct "middle path," because the more anxious we are, the more restlessness there is in our minds, and the more coarse the wandering thoughts will be. This will continue on and on like a brakeless train. If we investigate the wandering thoughts with the wisdom of the Buddhadharma, we will be able to see the patterns more clearly.

What do we do when we see that our mind is stuffed with wandering thoughts? It seems impossible to clean up the inner space. However, how do we clean a room that is filled with stuff and overly congested? We remove some items by the entrance, and then push off some big pieces to make a path for walking through and getting in.

Why do we study the Buddhadharma and practice seated meditation? It is to see our mind with clarity — seeing our wandering thoughts, our life, our personality, our strength, and also our weakness. When we understand and accept ourselves, we can understand all human beings, and we are then enabled to accept and tolerate others.

3

Concentration and Contemplation

In daily life, frequent occurrences usually leave deep impressions in our consciousness. Dwelling there for a long time, impressions firm up with feelings and turn into emotionally charged opinions or habits. When we need to respond to our surroundings, the habitual energy surfaces and our inclinations will gravitate toward it. This is karmic force pulling us toward its corresponding energy — just like people who enjoy spending time together often have similar interests or habits, or the places we like to go have something in common attracting us. These tendencies were generated in the past. In the cycles of birth and death, they have become influential. Through the observation of wandering thoughts, we need to see clearly what we have deeply stored, distinguishing between that which is wholesome and that which is polluted. With the practice of contemplation, we can penetrate and perceive the stains in our mind. Pollutants obstruct and cause us to sense turbulence so that we feel unease and mental pain. As the scripture says in Buddhism, "Observing the body, it is unclean; observing the feelings, they are suffering."

Strengthening Concentration

Observing feelings includes not only the sensations of the five sense faculties of eye, ear, nose, tongue, and body; our perceptions also have feelings, and these are deeper than bodily sensations. Sometimes we might be able to satisfy our body's cravings with "pleasurable" things, but inner feelings are more subtle and deep. What we feel internally has both delight and worry, which we call "happiness" and "suffering". If we examine suffering carefully, we will discover that there is too much worry in our mind. Our thoughts are often not about "future" or "present," not having to do with what will happen to us in the future or how to live comfortably in current conditions. Instead, we cling both to the good times of the past and also to unpleasant experiences in our memory. All worries, grief, bitterness, anger, and etc. are mixed up in our mind and become "suffering." Thus when we observe what is in our mind, we see aspects of wholesomeness as well as bitterness and pollution.

To a certain degree, applying the technique of calming or stilling without contemplation is limited to the function of concentration. When the ability to remain still is not yet firmly grounded, using such a technique certainly helps to collect our thoughts and prevent them from running all over the place. This is a practical way of guarding the sense gates since some wandering thoughts will entice us, and desires of the five sense faculties are easily drawn outward by external objects. When concentration becomes stable, the practice can gradually be oriented toward observing wandering thoughts.

Actually, in the practice of calming or stilling, the functions of concentration and contemplation operate in tandem. On one hand, we keep focused on the method, for example, being mindful of the breathing; on the other hand, we are clearly aware that we are sitting in meditation. We must be vigilant in keeping the awareness that "I am practicing." By constantly reminding ourselves it prevents the energy of concentration from being dispersed. If the power of concentration is insufficient, utilize the function of observation to help it, tirelessly bringing the attention back to the method. As the power of concentration becomes stronger and stronger, the functions of awareness and stillness will merge and operate simultaneously. When concentration is not being interrupted and the focus of contemplation is turned to observation of wandering thoughts, perception will have clarity. Before reaching this point, since concentration may not be steady enough, if we try to observe our wandering thoughts, we could easily follow their movement.

Typically we are aware primarily of body movement, and at the same time, our attention also moves with it since we are unable to focus on one object. For instance, when doing prostrations, we are aware of the repeated moves of the body, but if concentration is not strong enough, we may only be aware of the movements at some moments; at other times, the attention is with the outward flowing wandering thoughts. If we can truly remain focused on one object as we get up from sitting and do prostrations, the attention should be constantly with the movement of the body, and the function of awareness can then be present at all times and in all moving conditions. In daily life, we are usually in moving mode and rarely in stillness. Therefore we have the tendency to be aware of the body only in dynamic situations. We seldom relax for a period of time without the attention being scattered. This is why, in the process of learning calming or stilling, we emphasize the practice of concentration and focus our attention on one object.

Illuminating Awareness

The function of awareness and concentration are closely related. In everyday life when the five sense faculties come into contact with the world, awareness is activated and discrimination arises. The sense faculty, the object, and perception come together and there is the so-called "contact." The function of our awareness is there at all times; however, out of habit, it is unable to stay on one object but runs constantly with thoughts. Some practice methods help us to be aware of the process and movements of our own thoughts but this mere function of awareness is not yet contemplation. It is usually the case that only after the movement has taken place, do we become aware of it because it is so rapid.

With awareness, we notice all moving conditions around us, but often our attention does not stay with the movement. If our attention is truly concentrated, we will feel that the movement and the awareness are more and more in sync. This would indicate that the ability to be still is relatively solid or, to some extent, one is in a state of meditative absorption, or samadhi. Clear awareness can know the details of movement and inform us simultaneously. As the practice progresses, gradually we discover this kind of condition in meditation and grow more sensitive to sensations. For instance, when we are sitting, we find sound to be rather crisp or noise is much louder than usual. This is because we are focusing on one object. So when the sense faculties and objects come in contact, the awareness is very sharp — as soon as the contact takes place, the sense faculty swiftly responds.

Actually, the function of awareness is always sensitive and sharp. It is less obvious only because one of our sense faculties is distracted, sort of "not on duty." For example, when you are looking at something, a sound comes and your attention shifts to the sound. Then your total awareness is no longer as sharp as before, having been dispersed. But if your attention remains well focused, the sense faculties will be quite sensitive. In some instances, one notices that the sound did not reach the ear directly but contacted the whole body first and then reached the ear. Since sound is a wave in the air, when one is concentrated, the body remains sensitive and is capable of sensing even the slightest vibration. In such a subtle state, since the inner ear is a slight distance from the sound wave outside of the body, some people sense the sound wave reaching the body prior to hearing the sound. One is being heard on the inside while the other is being heard on the outside where the sound wave approaches the body first in the process. The interval is very tiny, usually not detectable. Only in deep concentration, when concentration and awareness are unified and the two functions complement each other, are sensibilities sharp like this.

When we are aware of an object, it is not the function of only one sense faculty — other sense faculties are also in operation. Take prostration as an example. It is not only the eye that is being aware but also the touch of the body. The same is true in walking meditation, where attention is put on the contact of the bottom of the feet. Both are functions of touch but compared to eyes, body contact is less obvious. Normally the functions of eye-contact or ear-contact are the easiest, especially the eyes — their contact is the widest. This is why when we do prostrations or walking meditation, our attention is easily pulled away by objects in the immediate environment. If our mind is concentrated, we will be able to follow each movement and sense every detail instantly. However, usually when we prostrate, we only notice the bigger movement of the body, and subtle movements remain unnoticed. The function of awareness is there all the time, and it is only because there is not sufficient focus that awareness seems to be absent or half asleep.

While both concentration and awareness may be present with the function of the first five sense faculties (the bodily sense faculties), samadhi, the state of meditative absorption, is only present with the function of the sixth sense faculty — perception, or mind consciousness. The methods that we usually practice are cultivating awareness only. People are usually in moving mode and the five sense faculties are in contact with external objects effortlessly. If awareness merely functions in moving states, it would be just a function of the five bodily sense faculties without the ability to generate samadhi. We must turn awareness into an internal function of perception. Only then can it generate samadhi, for it is impossible for samadhi to correspond with the functions of the bodily sense faculties. The bodily sense faculties do not have the capability of connecting past, present, and future. When having contact with an object, the function of the bodily sense faculties immediately arises and ceases, so samadhi is out of the question. Samadhi occurs when the mind is in a highly concentrated condition, often described as "single-mindedness." Because the function of perception can link past, present, and future, it enables concentration and awareness to continue and last over a period of time — only then will samadhi become a possibility.

As a state of single-minded concentration is reached, the function of awareness will also be enhanced. The strength of awareness will keep reminding us to recollect internally and concentrate. When the ability to concentrate is heightened, it enables the mind to be still and enter a state of samadhi. Only human beings have this particular function because a human has the ability to think and memorize. Other sentient beings are not endowed with such capabilities.

When our mind is inwardly collected and stabilized, the function of awareness can be used to observe wandering thoughts. We can see that our mind is tainted and there are many pollutants. We can also see that our mind is home to worry and anxiety and has the conditions of suffering. Upon further reflection, we discover that there is subtle dis-ease in our mind even though on the surface it appears fine. Sometimes we may seem to sit well in meditation but there always seems to be some feelings of concern or worry, and it is unclear what the worries are about. Not until we go deep and look, can we gradually uncover what causes these worries and this unease. This is the function of illuminating awareness or contemplation.

With contemplation, we see the thoughts that cause karmic effects and consequences, and we see perceptions of our mind that connect past, present, and future. From our own wandering thoughts, we see the manifestation of reality in our mind and can discern which streams are wholesome or unwholesome and why human beings transmigrate. Continuing our investigating and analyzing, we will realize that as long as there is arising, there is ceasing — ordinary people will fluctuate in samsara or suffering, enlightened beings will reach nirvana or liberation. To reach nirvana, we must take the path of the enlightened beings. Thus we can reason and comprehend the four fundamental right views in Buddhism — kindness and evil, karmic actions and retribution, past and future, ordinary people and enlightened beings.

Foundation of Practice

Having established the fundamental right view, you will understand the reason for practice. So when you are unable to apply the method in meditation, you will not be discouraged or feel that the aim of practice is too vague or remote because you see impurity and suffering in samsara. You know that, in order not to continue fluctuating in samsara, the path of the enlightened toward nirvana is necessary. You resolve to take refuge in the Buddhadharma and practice the Middle Path — a well-balanced approach without extremities — in order to realize the Way. When you return to everyday life and maintain such awareness, as you see your own life in samsara, you will ponder, "To continue the cycle like this? Where is the end?" Then you will understand with conviction that the ultimate goal of practice is liberation.

Human spirit is energy and has positive and negative aspects. The functions of consciousness are attached to the physical body, constantly working and flowing. When the body is gone, it is only the material aspect of energy that is gone. The spiritual aspect does not vanish and will continue on. From what you see about your past and future, you can comprehend what samsara is about in a real sense. Therefore, the ultimate goal is to free your mind from obstructions in the domain of samsara and be truly liberated.

Reading Buddhist texts and studying the Dharma can help you understand the essential doctrine and develop right view. It is illustrated in the Buddhadharma that there is right view of good and evil, right view of causes and effects, right view of past and future, and right view of ordinary and enlightened beings. Usually people consider such doctrine abstract or only apply it to what exists externally. When you begin to practice and are aware of your wandering thoughts, you can understand on a deeper level the meanings of these teachings and verify them with your own observations.

Usually these concepts and principles are treated as external phenomena and good and evil are seen as "out there." To most of us, karmic retributions are just consequences of bad deeds done by other people. But when you look at the wandering thoughts and their operations in your own mind, you can see directly the good and evil, causes and effects, past and future, and all varieties of phenomena. They clearly fluctuate in your mind. At such time you will understand keenly why life is a cyclic movement of samsara. From observation you know that the actions of good and evil have consequences. These karmic consequences float in the sea of samsara and will continue on. Some of the consequences immediately manifest in your consciousness. If you want their effects to be diminished or disappear altogether, you must turn to practice that is toward nirvana.

Mutual Verification

When we implement methods in practice, it is necessary for the methods to have a solid foundation on right doctrine or principles. Having right view of the Buddhadharma, we can verify the states of contemplation or insight. We use principles to understand the operations of wandering thoughts, confirming that the entire process is indeed as it is explained in the doctrine. From what we observe, we can also verify from our actual experience and reflect on the theory that we have learned. In such a way, interrelated principles and actual practice verify each other mutually. Then we have a more accurate and complete comprehension of doctrine, and our perceptions become more lucid and grounded. It will not be something others have told us but will be direct seeing, observing, and realizing through our practice.

The Buddhadharma states that "Observing the body, it is unclean" and "Observing feelings, they are suffering." Usually, our reflections feel like something outside. Only when we observe the conditions of our own mind, do we actually know it is complex and unclean and has lots of afflictions. Because of the afflictions, karmic actions take root and suffering is guaranteed. When you observe suffering in your mind, you know that it is from ignorance and karmic retribution, and that suffering is nothing more than karmic consequences. Suffering gives rise to new confusion, and new karmic action is taken and produces new suffering. So samsara continues on and on like this. When you see that samsara is truly suffering, you want to extinguish this suffering; the extinguishing of suffering is nirvana. Now the direction of your practice is clearer, and your confidence will grow stronger.

Sometimes we know only vaguely about the doctrine, or may not thoroughly comprehend certain parts of it. In some cases it is due to barriers in understanding the meaning of certain words. In other cases, it may be because the thinking process is not refined. When your mind is concentrated and settled in relatively subtle conditions, you can investigate deeply, and you may find some of the hard-to-understand doctrines you previously studied such as "Dependent Origination," "Emptiness," or "No-self" are now slowly making sense.

When trying to contemplate something profound and subtle, it is extremely beneficial to utilize the functions of meditative absorption or samadhi. If your mind cannot concentrate on one object or stay in a stable condition, there will be insufficient strength to penetrate. It is often the case that when we try to generate mindfulness and begin contemplation, we are distracted by wandering thoughts and therefore unable to go very deep.

Some of the methods of contemplation require us to have a good grasp of basic right views of Buddhism. However, views are still in the domain of intellect. We need to use what we observe about wandering thoughts to verify the theory. We may know the principles and use them in circumstances of life. Doing this, we can get a clue by categorizing them and observing how wandering thoughts operate. But this type of contemplation is not the most profound and is still within the relational scope of verification of theory and experience. What the theory talks about is the phenomena of life that are manifested and apparent. Nonetheless, such verification helps us to have a more accurate and deeper understanding with right view, and it heightens our confidence in Buddhist study.

Observing and understanding that the body is unclean and our mind is suffering is not yet liberation. Such contemplation only helps us to take one step towards departing from suffering. Further contemplation and penetration is necessary.

Contemplation of Wisdom

Contemplation in Buddhism is to contemplate all dharma or phenomena including the intrinsic nature of mind. What is intrinsic nature? It is no-self. We wish to know directly about no-self. However, in some — if not most — cases, we are unable to penetrate thoroughly and we need to perceive via observing impermanence, which helps us to see with crystal clarity the entire operation of body and mind — all phenomena included. Comprehending and realizing no-self is itself the nirvana of absolute emptiness or silence.

In the journey from samsara to nirvana, we must first learn about samsara; then we can further understand the necessity of attaining nirvana. Often people are not even aware of samsara, imagining that they will reach nirvana once they take up the practice. Without an understanding of samsara, there is no way to attain nirvana. Therefore we must thoroughly understand cause-and-effect in the human realm, which is demonstrated in the cause-and-effect of karmic action and suffering.

The path from samsara to nirvana is the path from ordinary beings to enlightened beings. This involves the causes and conditions of the supra-mundane dharma as well as the cycle of the twelve links of dependent origination. From the continuation and connection of good and evil, karmic consequences, past, present and future, we must see clearly our body and mind, the construction of this individual existence called "life," and the functions of cyclic transmigration. We cannot liberate others, but our own body and mind can be set free. Hence, in order to move toward nirvana, the practice of contemplation has to return to contemplating our own body and mind.

What we have studied in the doctrines of Buddhism helps us to see the transmigration of our body and our mind. The wandering thoughts reflect our body and conditions in our mind in living situations. The forming of wandering thoughts includes external conditions as well as biological functions, the five sense faculties, and also consciousness. All of these operate with the body and mind. If you can see clearly the constitution and transmigration of this body and mind, your desire or inspiration to practice will naturally arise. The more deeply you see, the stronger your belief will be, and the firmer your resolve to practice will be. The more you see the transmigration of yourself, the more you will know that you want to achieve nirvana in order to gradually alleviate the causes and conditions of samsara until they are totally extinguished.

The ultimate goal of practice must be liberation, and this requires a completely right view from the beginning. However, often we only know right view partially and are unable to integrate. We do not know the full spectrum of conditions of our body and mind or the operation and constitution of cyclic transmigration which can be seen in causes and effects in the mundane. In practice we can see them directly through observation and contemplation, and this can help us comprehend right view more completely. After establishing right view, we know more clearly what path to tread.

Sometimes we understand a certain theory but are unable to sense intimately how it is important to us. In studying Buddhism, many people read lots of books and can talk about it very fluently; but to them, the principles in the theory are not alive and do not have a feel of closeness — theory remains theory and the body and mind are still body and mind. So we must verify the authenticity of the theory through our body and mind. When we observe closely, what is revealed in the wandering thoughts and body and mind are what the doctrine tries to tell us. It is no doubt in accord with the phenomenon of samsara in the world of the mundane. Our body and mind transmigrate just like that. So theory is not something external, but neither does it exist objectively. When we truly observe and realize that the body and mind are suffering and impure, we can confirm that the body and mind belong to transmigration of the mundane and are not external, nor anything foreign. We often speak of the word samsara — thinking that it refers to other people who are suffering but not to ourselves while, in actuality, our entire body and mind are in transmigration. If we are certain that we have seen samsara, we can then further confirm that samsara can end. Then the faith to practice will arise.

How is faith established? From the process of samsara and with the Buddhist doctrine, we can investigate the world of the mundane, knowing that samsara is suffering and its extinction is possible. To stop suffering, it has to be done by this body and mind. In order to end suffering, it is necessary to follow the path of nirvana to a different world beyond. To extinguish samsara is liberation, and the way to accomplish this is to practice. To be on the right path, practice needs to be based on the principles of the supra-mundane, which is in conformity with the doctrines of impermanence, emptiness, and no-self. From the transmigration of causes and conditions we can see the true nature of causes and conditions. Dependent origination or conditioned existence is the principle of all phenomena. We see this nature through phenomena. This is the principle of dharma or phenomena, which is genuine, and is called the Noble Truth in Buddhism.

The core of the Noble Truth is no-self. Usually we cannot directly know what no-self is. Only through impermanence are we able to see clearly the operation of the body and mind as well as all phenomena. With the penetration to no-self, if we can actually realize the truth of it, it is itself nirvana. This is the Noble Truth. To practice according to the Noble Truth is the "Middle Path." Only by taking the Middle Path can we reach liberation.

Right speech, right action, and right livelihood in our daily life are the practices according to the Noble Truth. Usually we accomplish right speech, right action, and right livelihood according to the right view of impermanence and no-self. Then we reach right thought and right mindfulness and further achieve right meditation. After accomplishing right meditation, we proceed to realize nirvana, the ultimate goal that is based on right view. The entire practice is developed like this.

To build our practice solidly on the foundation of the Noble Truth, we must begin with observation and contemplation from our daily life. If we cannot see through our body and mind the suffering and impurity in samsara, we will not be able to establish right view of nirvana. Without understanding dependent origination through the construction of body and mind, it will be difficult to see the true nature of causes and conditions. If we cannot practice according to the true nature, which is enlightened, we will continue to transmigrate and remain in samsara.

The flow of good and evil, karma and retribution, past, present and future belongs to the realm of the ordinary or the mundane. To turn toward nirvana, we must practice according to the way of the supra-mundane. Our practice is the practice of our own body and mind. It is this body alive that is practicing. Having understood this, the theory and our body and mind will become close and intimate and will not be something alien. What we practice will not be something outside of the Buddhadharma but firmly based on the law and operations of the body and mind. This law is not something external at the far end of the universe. The construction and operation of our body and mind are based on such nature and laws. As long as there are causes and conditions of samsara, there will be causes and conditions of nirvana. And being so, our practice can be one of integration and therefore complete. When observing wandering thoughts, we are trying to see all of these clearly. Having seen them clearly, we will know how to proceed in the journey of practice.

4

Authentic Guide of Dharma

Earlier we've said that, as we quietly collect our thoughts and focus on the method, we will notice many wandering thoughts. Wandering thoughts usually disrupt our mind. To a certain degree, when we make decisions or react in daily life, habitual afflictions are often the dominant influence on our psyche and it is very easy for us to generate karma of suffering. Chan practice helps us to gradually increase the power of awareness and the ability to concentrate. If the practice is not yet solid, we try to focus on the method and let wandering thoughts arise and cease by themselves. When concentration becomes steady and the function of illuminating awareness is sharp, penetrating contemplation can be carried out with success.

Genuine Dharma as Signpost

When a certain state of concentration is reached, our mind will have strength to penetrate in contemplation. The power of concentration and contemplation can be utilized in observing wandering thoughts and investigating them thoroughly. By observing the movement of wandering thoughts we can perceive our life, our personality, the tendencies of our scattered mind, and we can make adjustments for the better. Sometimes this power can be so strong that it comes with a sort of super-knowledge or super-capability. In this case, one should be careful and not let this ability blindly exhibit as it pleases, for when our mind is concentrated and the strength continuously increases, if an "evil" thought arises, its damaging force can be immense. If one does not have genuine Dharma as the guide, it may happen that such power is abused and may result in actions that are governed by unlawful or unwholesome dharma. This is why some who are considered "achieved" practitioners can still make grievous mistakes. It is primarily because their practice is about cultivating meditative absorption, without wisdom as the guiding choice of their actions. Therefore, we emphasize that cultivation of samadhi should be informed by right views.

Genuine Dharma is like a thermometer for us. We will know if we have created unwholesome karma or have evil thoughts in our mind, for the suffering of anxiety or worry will be experienced. However, when unwholesome dharma is rampant, it is entirely possible that one may mistake suffering as pleasure. There are cases where people gladly perform evil-karma actions. The so-called happiness for them is that their desires are met to a certain extent, so they believe their actions are the right ones. As such acts are being conducted, there may be some sense of unease; however, it could be completely covered by overwhelming vexations at times. Even worse, because they gain some pleasant feelings of superficial satisfaction, out of ignorance, they will continue to perform the evil-karma actions.

Ignorance is lacking knowledge or having incomplete knowledge. When being in a state of not knowing, some may feel happy conducting unwholesome actions. When we were kids, what sort of naughty actions made us happy — burning ants, or catching fish, and watching animal fights? Some people enjoy watching horse races or cock-fights and treat this as a form of entertainment. But from the point view of the Buddhadharma, these actions are not deemed harmless. Therefore, if there were no ethical standards as guidance, many times we really would not know when our actions generate unwholesome impacts. Ignorance, of and by itself, is not evil; but it can very easily fall into the camp of evil deeds. Take someone who is physically or mentally disabled as an example. They know nothing or very little and they respond to the world sluggishly. They can be someone who is very simple but happy. However, it is also possible for them to become victims of evil.

When an evil thought arises in their mind, it can overwhelmingly influence all of their behavior. Sometimes people are really foolish and ignorant, unable to discern right from wrong, often considering something bad as good. In our everyday life, there can be times when we do not know where a clear boundary lies — we think we behaved according to the Dharma, but there are afflictions entangled in our mind and we are unable to truly discern. What we think is good or evil can often rely solely on the judgment of one thought! If this thought is based on right mindfulness, the action would be something good. Otherwise, it is directed by unwholesome dharma and something evil is created.

All psychological phenomena can have the characteristics of good, evil, or incognizant. In analyzing the human psyche, the principle of categorizing the phenomena of mind in Buddhism is wholesome or unwholesome. They determine whether our actions are in accord with wholesome or unwholesome dharma. If one did something not so good and regrets it afterward, it is a wholesome dharma. On the contrary, if one did something good and regrets it later, it becomes unwholesome dharma. For example, let's say you made a donation. When you go home and some stingy thoughts arise, making you regret and think, "Why did I give so much?" or "If I had known such and such earlier, I would not have given so much!" Thoughts like these fall into the category of unwholesome dharma. In the scripture Mahyāna-śatadharma-prakāśamukha-śāstra (Shastra on the Gateways to Understanding the Hundred Dharmas) or in the texts of Sectarian Buddhism, there are classifications regarding good and evil dharma of the mind. Having such references can help us to recognize wholesome dharma from unwholesome ones and vice versa.

In daily life we can also observe some commonly accepted ethical standards. Different communities, religions, and nationalities have their own codes of conduct concerning good and evil. Every individual also has personal belief in this respect. With such variety of criteria, when we make judgments, we can identify which are good or not, or which should be done and which should not. There are times when we may know something should not be done but we have no alternative but to do it. This is why the so-called laws or precepts in Buddhism are established in order to set rules for regulating people's behavior. Whether it is wholesome or unwholesome essentially depends on whether our action causes harm to others or not. Do not innocently think doing bad deeds only hurts other people. Actually it will also, for certain, cause harm to oneself.

The norms of the world, the values of religion, and regulations based on law can all help us to discern good from evil. If observation of wandering thoughts is based on Buddhadharma, it can be used to evaluate the thoughts. Those that cause bad karma should be eliminated, and wholesome thought or character of mind should be continued and encouraged to grow. When your mind becomes stronger and stronger, and function of illumination or contemplation becomes sharper and sharper, you will be able to make good judgments about the wandering thoughts, and make right choices according to the Dharma.

Strength of Mind

Ironically, in day-to-day life, things that we ought to do often cannot get done but those that should not be done are often accomplished. This is because the strength of our mind is insufficient, so it feels inadequate to make right choices. Particularly after we have started to study Buddhism, we may have some knowledge from the doctrine about worldly phenomena with their unlawful aspects and about wholesome and unwholesome dharma. But in reality, it is still very easy to fall into the trap of affliction and to make choices based on that.

For instance, you could be aware that, during this seven-day Chan retreat, you did not sit very well and you feel disappointed because you do not practice regularly at home in your daily life. So you decide to sit an hour every day when you go home after the retreat, hoping that in the next retreat you can sit better. You begin making plans — getting up at four o'clock each day and meditating; doing morning chanting and prostration at five and then having breakfast; after that going to work at seven; and reading Buddhist books for two hours after returning home from work. What happens then? The first day after returning home, you get up at four in the morning. The second day you feel a lack of energy, so you sleep one more hour and get up at five. As a result, only half an hour is left for sitting meditation and morning service is also reduced to half an hour. The third day, you get up at six, morning sitting and chanting are both skipped, and you are back to your old routine prior to the retreat. How strange! It was apparently well planned. Why, when it comes to implementation, does the energy not seem to be there? Well, it is because your mind has been influenced again by affliction.

Our practice must be enhancing the strength of mind so that the function of following the guidance of Dharma becomes the central force or dominating drive. If your mind is not the master, do not fantasize about liberating insight, for even managing simple affairs in daily life is out of your hands. If your mind is collected and has the power to concentrate, the ability to observe and contemplate will steadily increase, and only then can you be the master in your life. This strength of mastery can assist you in adjusting many aspects of your daily life.

Someone says, "My family situation is such and such and I can't help in changing it because my body does not listen to me!" Why does your body not listen to you? Because your mind is out of your control! If you have the power of self-mastery, you will realize that you have the ability to adjust and make amends. It is not that you forcefully change it, but seeing what needs to be done, you just take the initiative and do it. In many cases, situations in the family can slowly improve. For instance, you go home after this retreat, and your family members sense that something has shifted in you. When facing a problem, you are able to promptly make a choice and handle it with care and mindfulness, and you are more considerate of others. You family will sense the improvement in you, so next time when you wish to attend a seven-day retreat, not only will they praise and support you — better yet — they want you to go for a month! Since with only one week of practice you have already changed so much — they naturally think that if you went for a month, they would benefit so much more! Even when you do not want to go, they might encourage you to go by registering for you and praying that you will make it!

Obviously, the ability to be the master of oneself is very important. If you cannot be your own boss and your mind lacks strength, the environment will overwhelm you and you will not be able to make any adjustment. When your mind is able to concentrate and the power of self-mastery is increased, it will be possible to slowly influence the situation around you in a positive way.

Buddhadharma as Refuge

Taking refuge in the Dharma does not mean to have only knowledge of good and evil, or wholesome and unwholesome deeds, but also includes understanding the reasons and principles behind it. The Buddhadharma has a complete system of teachings for distinguishing good and evil. We can take these teachings as the foundation. It works just like professional organizations that have their own set of ethics, which are called "regulations of the profession".

People tend to think that many attorneys seem to be defending the bad guys most of the time. Actually in the legal profession, as long as there is someone who hires them, lawyers must work for them and are expected to provide excellent service. Whether this client is a good person or not is an entirely different matter. Since there is a body of legal ethics which serve as standards, from the lawyers' perspective, it is unprofessional if they do not do their jobs. What makes the judgment is nothing but the evidence. Even if someone is guilty, if the prosecutor is unable to present any evidence or the evidence is not sufficient to convince the judge and the jury, the defendant is ruled not guilty. The attorney of the defendant has the opportunity to refute each and every piece of evidence presented so that the prosecutor's case can become invalid. These are the ethical rules governing the profession of law and the lawyers must abide by them.

The same applies to religion. Different religions have approaches of their own to deal with good and evil. Some are distinctive even in fundamental doctrines. From the point view of Buddhism, some actions might be considered wrong, while based on another's discipline, there might be a whole system of theories demonstrating they are right actions. When we practice according to Buddhist discipline, we must take refuge in the Buddhadharma, learning what is good to do and what is not. Furthermore, we should know the reasons or principles behind these judgments and instructions.

Having a clear understanding of the Buddhadharma helps us to distinguish between good and evil more clearly. Take the precept of non-killing as an example. The Buddhist belief is that all sentient beings are a form of life. From the perspective of dependent origination, all beings are actually one body of the universe. All beings coexist on planet earth. If human beings intentionally kill any form of life or destroy an inhabitant or ecology of the environment, the harm eventually comes back to human beings themselves. If we observe non-killing based on such understanding, environmental protection can be carried out more naturally rather than enforcing it just because there is a so-called commandment requiring us to do so. This is why, particularly during contemplation, not only do we need to have the knowledge of discerning wholesome dharma from unwholesome dharma, but we must also understand the underlying principles. Only then, regardless if you contemplate on impurity, loving-kindness, or causes and conditions of dependent origination, as long as you know the correct applications of the principles and you have the energy to deeply penetrate, you will no doubt succeed.

The most common experience in practice is that there is too much affliction and too many wandering thoughts in our mind. This is the reason that, when things happen in life, it is usually affliction and wandering thought that lead us to make decisions. If we can collect our mind and concentrate, thinking with Buddhadharma and strengthening our mindfulness, letting the Dharma take root deeply in our mind, we will be able to stay in accord with the Dharma and afflictions will gradually lessen. Even if we do not dive in deeply, after a period of reading Buddhist literature and reflecting upon it, we will find that when we need to make decisions, it is effortless to evaluate the situation and make sound choices. Otherwise, if we do not read any Dharma books for a long period of time, our mind can slowly be covered by afflictions since our mind has had only surface contact with the Dharma, not actual realization, and rhe Dharma has not yet penetrated deeply into our being. Only after being influenced by the teachings of the Dharma can our actions be naturally in harmony with the Dharma. It is the same for followers of other religions. As they take in the teachings from their religion, their behavior will tend to gravitate toward that direction. So the Dharma is extremely important. We should practice in accordance with the Dharma by studying Buddhist scriptures and Dharma literature.

While contemplating on the Buddhadharma, the teachings will purify our mind. Being purified, comprehension of the Dharma will be more solid and steady. As the power of Dharma integrates and incorporates with our mind and becomes a dominating force, when it is time for decision-making, we can make it in accord with the Dharma instead of in accord with vexations. As our mind is being purified by the Dharma, it will definitely generate wholesome energy. Chan practice is precisely for cultivating such wholesome energy in our mind.

Integration in Practice

When the function of concentrated observation becomes established, we can contemplate and purify our mind with the Dharma. But this type of contemplation is still largely on the periphery as far as realization is concerned. Continuing with the process, though, we can see the core of the Dharma, which is impermanence and no-self. Should you be able to realize no-self, it will be true enlightenment, which is stopping the cycle of birth and death and is the end of suffering. If one can attain this level, in the whole process of contemplation, thinking itself will have tremendous clarity.

Once you have a deep understanding of the Dharma, you will be able to thoroughly integrate what you have learned and meditated about. In the process of deep investigation, much of what was unclear will start making sense. Much of what were parts and pieces before can now be connected. In the practice of calming and contemplation, as the function of illuminating contemplation becomes sharp, one can have realization about some profound teachings. For example, there are verses in the Heart Sutra that you did not comprehend before. Now when you look at them, you may be able to have a deep and thorough understanding.

Some Chan masters do not give their attention to theoretical parts of the teaching. If you ask them to explain doctrines or answer questions that are philosophical in nature, a few sentences may be all that will be given. Why? It is because they do not think in terms of theory. However, do not therefore imagine that these Chan masters have simply one koan (so-called "public case" in Chinese Chan literature) to fathom as their practice. It is simply not so. Their practice has a central doctrine, which is "all beings have Buddha-nature".

This is the concept of " intrinsic nature itself is purity". In every moment, they are practicing with this core teaching. They believe that saying too much will distract the students so they forgo the theory part and go directly to the core of the teaching. If your mind can focus with the ability of calming first, the function of contemplation will follow and at such a time, regardless whether you use Huatou (a key phrase for concentration or investigation) or other methods, you are likely to succeed fairly quickly. On the other hand, after having had enlightenment experiences, some Chan masters do still employ a complete teaching system with doctrines in guiding their students. Yet no matter how great an expert in theoretical disciplines one may be, to truly guide students in the teaching of a complete system, the master must have certain direct experiences of Chan. We can see that almost every single founder of a sect or school in the history of Buddhism is without exception a Chan master. All patriarchs have had genuine experiences of and true realization of Chan.

After reading many books, some scholars find Buddhist teachings not very useful in a practical sense or they feel spiritual power is lacking. However, the writings of those who have gone deep in practice or the patriarchs or masters who have had direct realization are very profound and thought-provoking, such as those of great master Zhiyi (in Shui Dynasty of China), whose writings have benefitted students enormously from ancient times to the present. When we read these classic texts and use the teachings or methods to comprehend the Dharma, we have no doubt that they can be applied to practice and daily life, and with great energy. This is because these classics are nothing but the direct experiences and realizations of these eminent masters in the process of their practice and enlightenment.

5

Inner Journey of Contemplation

Contemplation is the practice that the concentrated mind focuses on while in seated meditation. As the mind is stablized, if we observe the flow of wandering thoughts during meditation, we will be able to better understand the right views that the Buddhadharma has imparted to us. The doctrines of the Four Noble Truths (suffering, cause of suffering, extinction of suffering, the path to extinction of suffering), Dependent Origination (or Conditioned Arising), and the Four Foundations of Mindfulness all have a ground of inference. When concentration and awareness have developed and reach the unified function of the mind, contemplation based on these doctrines can become lucid and direct. However, true comprehension of the Buddhadharma entails detailed reflection on the principles as well as realization in action, and it involves continued purification of the mind. In other words, understanding of the doctrines can be deepened only through actual practice.

Watching out for This Mentality

Our behaviors reflect the degree to which our practice has evolved or progressed. As Buddhadharma becomes the central stream of our thoughts, there will be a significant change or shift in our views and perceptions. When our practice progresses, our attitude and manner will be refined, the energy of

Dharma is strengthened in us and becomes a practical function, and we will have the capability to take action that is grounded in the Dharma. Our living situation will also adjust accordingly. This will all be naturally exhibited in our daily life.

Sometimes right mindfulness can be heavily covered by afflictions. For example, we may inflate ourselves and pretend to be an accomplished practitioner, bragging about such and such abilities of meditation which in fact we do not possess. This type of affliction reflects foolishness and, of course, greed. We crave and cling to worldly fame and gain, and therefore wish to present ourselves as someone who is regarded by others as a person of great achievement. We have only two cents in terms of depth in practice, but we want to demonstrate that we have five and seven cents — the extra pennies are phony. How long can such pretense last?

When there was an earthquake in Taiwan on September 21, 2009, some houses that were built on empty oil tanks immediately collapsed. It is the same with people. If your practice is based on too many of these empty tanks, the slightest shake will cause it to collapse. You may consider yourself deeply trained in meditation or other aspects of practice, but as soon as someone criticizes you with strong words, your empty tanks show themselves as faces of rage. Thus, achievements in practice cannot be fabricated. Sometimes we do not really know ourselves, and this is why some practitioners often make faulty claims that they have reached certain states in meditation. In Buddhism, this type of hindrance is called "elevated arrogance".

After sitting for a while, some meditators may feel there is something subtle moving inside, and they think they have "gotten it" in terms of enlightenment, or perhaps have entered the first dhyana state (deep meditative absorption). Having had a few reoccurrences of this sort, they think, "This is already the fourth time. It must be the fourth dhyana." There are also practitioners who believe that they have attained the "fruit" (status rank in realization). They mistake non-real as real without knowing it and claim that they have attained such and such. Why? They want to show off that they are in higher states of practice. To be honest, if an experience can be expressed in words, it is very shallow. Should someone's practice truly reach a great depth, it would be very difficult for one to describe it when asked.

You may go to a teacher or friends for discussion about a state that appears in meditation to find out if they have experienced it. However, having gained knowledge about such an occurrence, it is best to put it down and not cling to it. If you indulge in publicizing it to a wider audience, the more you speak about it, the more attached you will become and the more you will desire these experiences. Consequently, you will be in trouble. On one hand, you will not likely make further progress in meditation. And on the other hand, you will try to force the state to happen. As you try to force it, you will only be pacing up and down in the very same place. You might tell yourself, "Quick! Quick! Quick!" Yet, after racing for a while, you are still in the same place without moving an inch — You have only made the endeavor noisy while imagining your practice got a trophy. When you speak with others about your achievements, it always corresponds with arrogance and greed. The more you talk about it, the deeper the clinging goes. Such a corrupt condition will manifest without difficulty because it has become your habit.

During sitting meditation, you may be excited when energy in the body moves and you cannot help but tell other people, "I had such and such movement today." Tomorrow another motion pops out and you again tell others. But what does such and such movement of your body do anyway? We are practicing "quiet sitting meditation", not competing for "moving meditation"! If there is chi (flow of subtle or vital energy) moving in your body, eventually it will quiet down and the body will return to sitting quietly. If chi flows smoothly, the spontaneous movement will stop by itself. Only when it cannot flow smoothly does it dramatically move around in the body. A well-adjusted body can experience energy shifts which flow unimpeded. When this happens, where did your moving chi go? Sitting meditation does not require deliberate use or manipulation of chi because, after all, we are not in a chi-gong class!

Naturally, where one's practice is in terms of depth does not need to be concealed. Neither does it need to be decorated and exhibited to the public. If your practice goes well and others want to learn about it, you may share it if you have good teaching skills. What you share with others may be aspects or features that are general and common in meditation process. In the classic works of Great Master Zhiyi, he mentions characteristics about the manifestation of good-root and evil-root. However, when you speak about the conditions or states that appear in practice, part of it is your own unique experience. Some of it is what you have learned from discussions with others. Another portion is what you have read and understood from the scriptures or treatises on the subject. What we are trying to point out is that some practitioners enjoy demonstrating their achievement in practice to other people. Actually, it is better not to talk about it when it can be avoided unless you are unclear about something in the course of practice, in which case, you may wish to ask someone for clarification or advice. Then together you may explore and investigate. It is not prohibited to learn in this way in order to facilitate progress with one's practice.

Practice is totally an inner journey, not something to wear on our sleeves. Thus, when practicing with diligence, just simply practice. Where the cultivation takes you will manifest naturally in due course. If it is being decorated, that soon will be revealed. In retreats, some women will not dare to let others see them with washed faces. If the wake up call is at three o'clock, they will get up at one to apply makeup. Only with makeup are they willing to show up in the morning. If lights-off is at ten o'clock in the evening, they might go to sleep after midnight because they need to wash off the layers of makeup! Why bother with such labor? In the evening, a handful of water to wash off the face and go to bed is simple enough. In the morning, it is the same — a handful water to refresh the face and there you are — on your cushion in the Chan hall! Can't we be just simply clean while sitting in the Chan hall? The truth is, some people do not like their own "original face". Only when they have covered it with colors and paste do they feel pleased.

Attitude and mentality before meditation practice is very important. Having basic understanding about right view of Buddhism, we keep adjusting our speech and behavior in daily life in order to stay in harmony with the Dharma. This is the real cultivation. In the process, we discover our own weaknesses or sometimes we go astray. But in either case, right understanding of the Dharma can help us gradually get back on track.

Getting Closer to the Dharma

As the mind gains strength through meditation, you will have the power of self-mastery, and the ability to contemplate is also heightened. However, often you sit there, not knowing on what you should contemplate. Why is this the case? Because you are not yet clear about the Dharma, and you have no idea where to start your contemplation. Although the periphery of contemplation at the beginning is still within the scope of theory, it is useful nonetheless. Begin with theory and continue to penetrate. Gradually you will become acquainted with the original nature of all phenomena. In fact, the theory is meant to communicate such information. Perceiving the nature of phenomena is a journey through theory.

Of course, theory is merely theory. It must be tested in your practice and your practice must confirm the theory. Only then can you truly see and therefore understand the profound teachings of the Dharma. During such a process, you will find that your mind is getting closer and closer to the Dharma. In daily life your actions will also exhibit harmony with the Dharma. When your mind abides in depth, it generates a subtle force that enables you to stay away from unwholesome conduct.

For example, from the classic texts we have learned that those whose spiritual attainment has reached the stage of the so-called "Initial Fruit" or "Stream Enterer" in terms of enlightenment are those who are far from killing. There are descriptions in the scriptures stating that when "Stream Enterers" dig in farming activities, insects would stay at least four inches away from them. This explains why, when those whose practice has attained certain levels sit and meditate in open places in the wild, there is absolutely no need for them to worry. Ordinary practitioners would probably feel terrified in those locations. Why? Ordinary practitioners would fear that the "good friends" — wild animals or insects — might come and find them. They fear this because they have too many worries, attachments, and emotions of hatred.

Chan masters do not worry about these types of things. Their spirit has reached the state where there is a highly refined sensitivity. They can be with the wild animals with ease because they have no thought of hurting them. When ordinary people see these wild animals, they might shiver and be compelled to defend themselves. When a thought of fear or terror arises in the mind, animals can sense it so they will attack first in order to protect themselves. This is similar to what we see in everyday life — those who feel a lack of security have a tendency to be aggressive — the so-called "offense is the best defense".

Letting Go of Grabbing

Contemplation is a process of simplification, but human beings love to continuously seek outwards, wanting this and that. The condition of seeking in mind has a compulsion to grab. For instance, when you first begin to practice, you grab hold of your breath, as if without grabbing the breath, your mind has no place to put itself. Afterwards, being worried that it is not tight and steady, you use counting to help seize the breath a bit more securely. One, two, three times, and the breath slowly stabilizes; so you let go of counting and remain with the breath. But for some people, as soon as they drop the count, breathing loses stability immediately. This is due to the instability in the mind, and therefore the breathing behaves in the same way .

Should your practice go well and breathing become more and more refined, you will find the in and out of the breath is a subtle movement. You can think of the breath as a point and settle your attention on it. However, when you practice with vigilance, sometimes you can still feel empty and your mind is absent. It is as if something has been lost in sitting and you want to grab something. So you might try to look for your breath and make it coarse in order to continue counting. Without anything to hold on to, it seems that without the habit of grabbing, you do not know what else to do. If what you have in your mind is too tiny, you will want to catch something big. In daily life, what do you grab? Are you accustomed to wanting and acquiring this and that? Is what you grab the real thing? No. What you have grabbed are your own desires. The desire in your mind is to want this and that, so you go and seize it. What you catch are external things, but you do it with your mind, your desire, and your afflictions.

Now you must slowly make adjustments, learning to let go both of things and of grabbing. The method to do this is very simple — stay with your breath and then stay with your stillness. When you focus on this one point, you will feel stable and fulfilled, and you will not want to look for something out there to fill the void. You will be able to continue to be at ease with this one object and practice.

Obstacle of Drowsiness

If your concentration becomes stronger and stronger and awareness remains relatively feeble, it is possible that you may slowly enter a deep state of meditative absorption. But when awareness and concentration are equally strong, the function of concentration will supplement awareness to remain alert, and the two can develop uniformly. Thus in terms of meditative absorption, Buddhist practice emphasizes the fourth dhyana, for in the state of the fourth dhyana, the functions of concentration and awareness or illumination are equalized. Before entering the type of meditative absorption that is in the realm of form, awareness is relatively strong and the mind still seeks and clings to external objects at all times.

Whether observing wandering thoughts or pondering the meanings of the doctrines, what it refers to is still within the domain of the mundane. Only in the realm of form is awareness very active. When one enters a state of samadhi, the mind will not be as active but its function is still there and can be heightened with contemplation in single-minded dhyana. In such a state, regardless of whether you contemplate the external objects at the present moment or the nature of dharma, the mind will be powerful. But if you enter deep samadhi, awareness will be lessened and contemplation is not easy to carry out.

In this stage of practice, an obstacle that typically appears is drowsiness. At the beginning it is coarse. For example, when you are sitting, you doze off and the body sways which is obviously noticeable. In most cases, it is likely that your body is not well adjusted in daily life and the quality of your sleep is not good, or it is simply a habit. But sometimes it is just a transitional condition. Especially after a meal, it is easy to feel sleepy. So during the first sitting period after lunch you feel heavy-eyed, but the second period is easier.

When you feel sleepy, do not resist it. Have a good nap. When you wake up, this type of lethargy will pass. Drowsiness has a time span. Sometimes you may counteract this at the time of sitting. When there is a sign that you might fall asleep, just raise a thought and let the brain wake up. Sometimes you may still feel sleepy until the third or fourth period of sitting. Why is this so? Maybe your body is too tired or exhausted. If you are doing well with the method, it consumes a great deal of energy and may cause the body to tire. In this case, the most comfortable thing might be to lie down and sleep, allowing the whole body to relax. However, in the Chan hall this cannot be accomodated. So you sit there and nod your head a few times, giving it a good release. The drowsiness will pass. This type of drowsiness is manageable by making adjustments.

For some people, however, as soon as they take the cushion to sit, drowsiness arrives. This is likely related to certain physical conditions or partially due to stress from life situations or work. Every part of their body seems to feel tense. Even when asleep, their body is still unable to relax and often these people will have dreams. So their sleep is very shallow. When they need to work the next day, they have to rely on stimulants to stay awake. Being unnaturally stimulated, their bodies become tense. Even if they take a nap, they are unable to have good quality sleep. This situation needs a longer time to resolve in daily life. Thus, in order to sleep well, one must be at ease in the mind and relaxed in the body.

There is another way to relax which is to massage all toes before going to sleep. It will help the entire body to relax. The most easily tensed parts of the body are the toes. When the toes are relaxed, the whole body relaxes. There have been some reports saying that it is beneficial to wear socks for five to ten minutes before taking them off for sleep. This will let the feet be warm so one can sleep well. In China, there has actually been a widely spread life-conserving "recipe" or technique, which is soaking the feet. Many old people soak their feet with warm water to help with sleep. If one can sleep well, the symptom of drowsiness will be diminished.

When your practice goes well, it will also reduce the chances of lethargy. But sometimes drowsiness appears when your practice is going smoothly. For example, at a certain stage, the concentration is too powerful and one can all of sudden lose awareness — the mind suddenly drops or has a sense of "fall"!

This happens only when your method is working for you very well. Otherwise, you would not have such an incident. After this has passed, you do not feel tired. Instead, you feel quite energetic because just before it happened, your mind was extremely concentrated. Your practice is basically solid. Awareness lapsed only for a brief moment. What happened was that in practice, the function of concentration and awareness coordinate with each other. But when you have too many thoughts and are trying with full force to pull the mind back to the method, you strengthen the function of concentration, so for a moment, awareness seems lost.

If you feel drowsy when you count the breath, most often such drowsiness is rather coarse. When you stop the counting and just follow the breath for a while, you may all of sudden "fall" as if you were falling asleep and then wake up. You know you are working on the method, and awareness disappears for only a brief moment. Actually, without awareness your body will fall down. As long as you keep employing the method, this condition will also slowly pass.

Sometimes there are signals before drowsiness appears. You do not notice them because they pass too quickly. If you ignore the signals a few times and continue to concentrate and slowly raise the function of awareness, your sleepiness will pass. This type of drowsiness is not considered stupor. It is only losing awareness. If in daily life the body is not well adjusted, the practice of training the body and cultivating the mind does not coordinate well. Your mind can lose its awareness and the body will "drop" for an instant without falling down. If the body is well maintained in daily life, and the method of breathing is well utilized, the practice will steadily progress.

Actually the method of counting breaths can help increase awareness and enter the stage of "following breath". However, if you often lose awareness as you concentrate, you may slip into a state of stupor and your mind falls into a state of incognizance. This is in the category of stupidity and it is not ideal. In such a state your mind has lost consciousness and is unable to be aware of anything. Without the function of differentiation, the power of awareness is asleep. Not only can this occur in deep absorption, it can also happen occasionally in shallow states of meditation. Hence, in diligent practice, one must constantly keep awareness functioning.

True Contemplation

Contemplation is grounded in awareness. It is a function of conscious thinking. Usually the thinking process only involves having access (listening or reading, etc.) to the Dharma and reflecting on it. When you practice based on the principles of single-minded meditative absorption, it is different from the usual sense of thinking. In contemplation, while thinking is in the arena of dhyana, the process enters the stage of cultivation of wisdom. In other words, at this stage you already possess right view and are able to discern and differentiate from the phenomena of good and evil in coarse form on the surface to the subtle domain of essence which is the original nature of all phenomena.

At the time of Shakyamuni Buddha, there were some philosophers, non-Buddhist practitioners (whose practices are referred as "outer path") or heretics, who were meticulous thinkers and had certain wisdom. However, that wisdom was not considered ultimate by the Buddha because it did not perceive the nature or characteristics of dharma. When these people wanted to learn from the Buddha, as long as they did not do so with the spirit of competing and winning or overly clinging to debate, the Buddha simply pointed out the truth and they comprehended his teachings effortlessly. There were others who indulged in public debate and often liked to argue with the Buddha. The Buddha did not argue with them. Rather, he simply gave them reasons or principles. Upon hearing the Buddha, they were enlightened, particularly those Brahmans who often discussed doctrines with him. It was often the case that, with only a few verses or sentences, the Buddha solved their problems or corrected subtle but erroneous views. Many of them took refuge and became Buddhists as a result of these interactions.

As long as we practice according to the Dharma, the thinking process will gradually enter more subtle and deeper arenas of discernment. At the beginning of contemplation, we may tend to pay attention more to the logic and reasoning of the doctrine, verifying these with our understanding from experiences. But in the end, it has to mesh with the core — the nature of dharma or phenomena. By observing impurity of the body and suffering of our mind, we understand the essential Buddhist point of view, which says that there are the principles of wholesome and unwholesome, karma and retribution, past and future, ordinary and enlightened beings. To enter the path of the enlightened, we must turn away from the entrance of samsara and enter the gate of nirvana. In order to do this, we must advance to the practice of contemplation on the nature of all dharma.

Contemplation on the nature of dharma is centered on "no-self". Usually it is not an easy task to directly investigate "no-self". So we first get in the door by contemplating impermanence. This begins by observing that our mind is changing all the time and is devoid of any self-existing entity called "self". Everything in the universe changes constantly. The impermanence we commonly see in daily life is more apparent but some changes are less obvious. Only when something drastic happens do we wake up to what is called "impermanence".

It always feels like we do not change much, while every year and every day we are changing. You can see that from photos you take every year. Of course nowadays technology is so advanced that we can use computer software to edit the images. For example, it is very popular nowadays for newlywed couples to make a wedding album. In the photos, the eyebrows of the bride are trimmed thin and long. If you put the photos next to the actual person, it is hard to see that they are the same person. And it is difficult to determine if the real person is prettier or the image in the photo is more beautiful. It is hard to say. If you say the image in the photo is more beautiful, it would be hinting that the bride herself is not so beautiful and only the photo editing made her look beautiful. In some cases you know she has changed in appearance, but it is not so obvious to be able to tell how. Or after a few years without seeing her, when you meet each other you think "Wow, how come she has aged so much!" But do not forget, when you see others looking older, you yourself have also aged. Often we only see others becoming old but do not see ourselves aging. Our body and mind are changing all the time. The change in mind is much faster than the body; however, it is not as readily perceivable because of our attachment to the past.

Impermanence is a continuously changing process — the "before" and "after", the "arising" and "ceasing", all have continuity. Let us use the analogy of a candle. When burning, it seems that there is not much difference in the flame, but in actuality it has been changing. If we imagine cutting it into pieces, what burns in one instant is not the same piece of candle that burned in the instant prior, and the latter burning cannot take place without the former burning because they are successively one and not separated — only the ceasing of the first instant has brought about the second instant of burning.

The so-called "uninterrupted continuity" refers to the operation of mind in continuous fashion — one incidence of arising and ceasing brings forth that of another. Take the flow of water as an example. We can see that a wave is pushed up by another wave, and this "other" wave is pushed by yet another wave. They continue without an individual unchanging body but only with the constant arising and ceasing. We look, look, and look, and still we do not perceive impermanence. But if those who have sharp "karmic roots" look at this phenomenon of impermanence, they might have an enlightenment experience. Another example is listening to the sound of water flowing, which is as if it is a single sound only. Actually in that sound, there are many sounds before and after. When we listen to rain, if the sense faculty of the ear is listening without mind discrimination, we can really hear the sound of the raindrops dropping one after another. The vibration of sound waves is the same. If we can hear it in fractions of an instant, we will realize impermanence. If we use our mind to distinguish it, the discriminative process connects past, present and future and makes it as if we only hear a single sound. If we listen only with the ear without the mind discriminating, we can hear the sound of each micro-instant and therefore understand impermanence.

It is the same for mindfulness of the breath or walking meditation. Usually our attention is put on the foot that is touching the ground. Another way is to observe the foot that is moving. In the beginning we observe a single step as a process of one arising and ceasing. Then, from the bigger movement of arising and ceasing, we see smaller ones. When we walk slowly, it becomes more and more subtle. If we walk with big steps, just hastily walking and walking and walking, we cannot see the arising and ceasing clearly. It is the same with prostration. If our mind is still, we can see that the movement is actually a series of connected motions.

Typically, our contemplation only involves awareness of the motions without contemplating the Dharma. Only when we contemplate the Dharma can we see the nature of arising and ceasing in phenomena. From the phenomenon of arising and ceasing, we understand and realize impermanence. If we see the movement of what is happening, it is merely the function of awareness. We need to perceive impermanence from seeing arising and ceasing, or using the doctrine of impermanence to verify our experience of the phenomenon. Such is contemplation. Hence, behind contemplation there must be the Dharma. If during contemplation we are merely aware of movements or sounds, they are still the functions of the sense faculties of eye or ear or body. They are awareness but not real wisdom.

Some people think that being aware of the arising and ceasing of wandering thoughts, the breath, and movements of the body is perception of the causes and conditions of the moment. In fact, we are unable to perceive real causes and conditions of the present moment unless our mind is extremely refined. When our mind is in a refined condition, it can see arising and ceasing on a micro-level, instant by instant. Right then and there, we must verify directly the perception of phenomenon with the nature of impermanence and no-self.

With the insight of impermanence we can see why phenomena are constantly changing. Everything is a combination of causes and conditions which is why nothing remains constant. With the understanding of no-self, we verify the truth of the original nature of all phenomena. Then we truly perceive the path. This is the practice of contemplation. When contemplation is very subtle, we can see each moment with exceeding clarity and intermesh with it. When achieving such realization, the attainment is genuine wisdom of the supra-mundane and true realization of no-self.

When you contemplate, you can also use the characteristics of no-self to verify phenomena, or vice versa. In this way, doctrine and experience verify each other mutually, and you will find that they get closer and closer to each other. When they completely mesh, it is realization or so-called enlightenment.

Realization of the Path is a transformation, a very rapid occurrence, and afterwards it is irreversible. It is irreversible because we have already crossed beyond the domain of the mind of birth and death and cyclic existence. The mind then lives in the present, settled with ease in the causes and conditions of the moment. Causes and conditions arise and cease very rapidly — they pass and, in the operation of phenomena, they move on. The mind does not dwell in the past or in the future, only residing in the present moment without expecting the next instant because as the present cause and condition is fulfilled, the next instant will naturally arise. As soon as the instant of the past is over, it is dropped. What has ceased will not arise again. Then the cycle does not continue.

However, since our mind is coarse, what we contemplate is usually that which has already happened. This is why when we prostrate, what we see are movements that have finished. How can we live in the present? We might think we are living in the present. We take the movement of the prostration as present, thinking what we see are causes and conditions of the moment. However, when concentration of the mind is so subtle, we can see every move and we can feel mind and movement are in sync — the thought and action seem to stick together as one. Such a state is supreme samadhi. But we need to further contemplate the intrinsic nature of all phenomena. Without this, it cannot be genuine enlightenment. At this stage, the function of concentration and awareness is very sharp and sensitive. The mind is with every movement. When meditative absorption can function like this, contemplating impermanence, no-self, and emptiness will lead to the experience of enlightenment.

Now we are still in the phase of rudimentary training. When we increase both the power of mastery and the ability to contemplate, we contemplate the true nature of phenomena. Then the mind is generally anchored on something rather deeply so if we, for example, hear an outside sound, it feels like a sound in the ground of consciousness. Should the sound feel like it is coming from the outside, one will be unable to enter samadhi. Regardless of what is being contemplated, be it sound or breath, it must be turned from the external object condition to an internal object condition. Only then can meditation enter the state of samadhi.

We are accustomed to clinging to things. Therefore, at the beginning of contemplation, the external object condition is of the first five sense faculties. The practice of mindfulness of the breath uses the sensation of the body and it is still external. When we observe something subtle, we may feel that breath is not a function of the body but rather a function in consciousness. Or in concentration and stillness, we may feel the focal point is not the nose but it has become an image in consciousness. If our mind has settled on the internal object condition, we can contemplate the arising and ceasing of thoughts.

Illumination of Wisdom

In Burmese dhyana practice, there is a method of contemplating the objects of aggregates. It categorizes the body into different types. It is a very subtle and complex process of contemplation. First it analyzes the elements of earth, water, fire, and wind. Then it proceeds to observing form, sound, smell, taste, and touch. The main purpose of this method is to help break attachment to what we know as the "self". Each manifested cause and condition is a body of composition. If you can analyze the body this way, in the end you will find it is impermanent and without any substance referred to as "self".

When you enter stillness, you can contemplate phenomena and the principle that the objective condition of dharma is devoid of self. This is taught in Buddhism, "Contemplating dharma, it is devoid of self." See that every thought is a composition of things and it is impermanent. When you can see clearly the subtlety of the arising and ceasing of thoughts, you will be able to see the phenomenon of compounding. At the end of the investigation, you will find that there is nothing unchanging. Just like a banana tree — as the bark is peeled off layer after layer, in the end, there is no center. You understand then that no-self is just like that.

To practice in accordance with the original nature of dharma and to contemplate it requires a solid foundation of understanding the doctrines and principles. If right view is absent, it is impossible to penetrate deeply and thoroughly. One must begin from study and reflection to comprehend the core of the profound truths —impermanence, no-self, and emptiness. Each and every one of the myriad of dharmas has intrinsic nature or characteristics, and the characteristics of all dharmas in essence are the same and not some self-existing entity like atman in Hinduism.

Contemplating the original nature of dharma means perceiving that the mind is constantly changing and that dharma has no self. This is contemplating the original nature. In order to successfully contemplate this, one must have a clear understanding of the concepts. Thus practice is not accomplished by simply sitting on the cushion and deliberate thinking. It has the prerequisite of study and reflection. From there one investigates the aggregation of the five skandas (form, feeling, conception, volition, and consciousness); that they are compound and empty without eye, ear, nose, tongue, body and perception, and there is no form, sound, smell, taste, touch, and dharma. Then you examine the body and the functions of its elements. Through segmentation, you see that there is nothing that is the so-called "I". Then you can understand emptiness. This is to first establish right view through study. Based on meditative absorption of single-mindedness, you then use experience to verify the theories from your study or vice versa. Slowly they mesh with each other more and more closely and reach the state of "free of hindrance". Then you have realized the wisdom of no barrier between doctrine and experience.

When you contemplate no-self, if you only sit there and think, "there is no self; there is no self," such practice will not do it because it is not based on theoretical foundations. When entering contemplation, we are not trying to analyze what no-self is, but rather to know that no-self is the original nature of all phenomena. You use this understanding of no-self to verify the condition that you are observing, or use the condition to verify the doctrine. Such is true contemplation. As long as your practice is solid, even if you did not really realize it in an experiential way, your ideas and views will gradually change and go through a transformation. In the process of your continued investigation of no-self and being infused by the permeating Buddhadharma, your mind and the theory become closer and closer. Since you are confident about the teaching, many areas of daily life will adjust for the better accordingly. Such is wisdom, although it is not the wisdom of supra-mundane.

With wisdom, when you make judgments or take actions, they will be different from when you did not have wisdom. From the twelve links of causes and conditions, we know that before a contact is initiated, it needs the six stations which are the six sense faculties of eye, ear, nose, tongue, body, and mind, or the six consciousnesses of sight, sound, smell, taste, touch, and idea. And in the six stations, there are material and non-material forms, which include perception. All of these compound together to form a body of life.

The first five sense faculties cling to external objects; then there is the function of deliberate or conscious thinking. The sense faculties, the objects, and the perceptions together become contact; and contact will generate sensations and feelings. If, when there is contact and you are in accord with ignorance, ignorance will cause craving, followed by clinging, becoming, birth, aging and death. If it is in accord with wisdom, right at the moment of contact, ignorance ends and craving ceases, and all others that follow in the chain will be extinguished. The functions of clinging and becoming will not arise. At the instant of contact, what the sense faculty of eye contacted is no longer an eye-perception but wisdom, which is often termed as "turning perception to wisdom".

Wisdom illuminates all these manifested phenomena with the compounding functions, and also illuminates the nature of all phenomena. If all are extinguished right in the moment, the cyclic flux of samsara is also extinguished. Although our wisdom cannot stop samsara, it can at least slow it down or diminish its power. Usually once there is contact, an action immediately rushes out because it is directed by ignorance. Consequently this action will − for certain − resonate with afflictions. However, if a contact takes place, and the function of awareness arises immediately, as soon as you sense the arising of afflictions, you use wisdom to shed light on it. This can slowly tame the afflictions.

Sometimes there are problems when an object contact takes place and, because the power of concentration is lacking, there is no way for wisdom to arise. If the function of illumination is absent, then simply go back to the breath. This is the technique − no matter what happens, when you feel emotional turbulence, return to the breath, pay attention to the breath, slowly breathe in and slowly breathe out. Repeating it a few times, breathing will slow down and the heartbeat will also slow down. Our breath reflects the conditions of our body and mind. When breathing is smooth and refined, mind will also be regulated. Under such conditions, your handling of what happens will be different. The function of awareness and the thoughts that we observe can enable a bright mind to arise when we come in contact with objects. If we can practice in daily life, it will diminish the flow of the cyclic force of suffering. Focusing on the breath and returning to breath is the method of stilling. As the mind becomes tranquil, then begin contemplation. This is the practice of stilling and contemplation.

Often, because it is covered by afflictions, our mind lacks strength. We need to continue practice for a long time to train our mind. Only then can it become sharp and the power of mastery enhanced. Then you can see with clarity the causes and conditions at the present moment, and you reduce the generation of unwholesome karma. With less evil karma being generated, when you sit, there will be fewer wandering thoughts. With fewer wandering thoughts, your mind can be more refined. And when you return to everyday life, less evil karma will be created. Then it becomes a wholesome cycle.

Thus, practice is not that you sit there and wait for entering samadhi or for enlightenment. If you keep wondering, "Why hasn't the state of enlightenment come yet? Why have I not become enlightened? How come I have not entered the first dhyana?" You sit there and wait and wait... when will you stop waiting? In the school of Chan there is a saying, "Wait until the year of the donkey." Why is it the year of the donkey? Because in the animal symbols of the Chinese zodiac system, there is no such year as that of the donkey! So, do you want to wait for the year of the donkey? It is up to you.

6

Realization of Wisdom

Contemplation involves comprehending profound truth. As we look into impermanence, no-self, and emptiness in a deeper and more subtle way, we will gradually have a grasp of these doctrines. The truth in them continuously purifies our mind, which will gradually become in sync with the Buddhadharma. Analyzing these subtle aspects has certain impacts on our thinking; however, it is still only knowledge or intellectual understanding. It must be transformed into wisdom by our observing and applying these doctrines in daily life and realizing or experiencing the truth.

Perceiving Impermanence

Usually we are only able to observe impermanence through external forms, which are often things that are coarse. The Buddha often uses the approach of "Emptiness of Easy Comprehension" to help us understand the profound truth of emptiness. He draws analogies from worldly phenomena that change rapidly to describe impermanence, such as "a bubble vanishes quickly", "lightning passes in a split second", or "in the morning there is dew on the grass, but when the sun comes out, it evaporates and disappears". There is a famous Chan verse that says, "Like a dream and reflection of a bubble, like dew on grass and lightning". We can see these changes in life. In order to observe subtle changes of a phenomenon, there must be a certain degree of meditative absorption. If one's mind is not refined enough, contemplation cannot go deep but will only remain on the surface.

When we see someone who dies at the age of eighty, we feel this phenomenon of impermanence lasts a very long time. If a baby dies just a few days after birth, we think impermanence is very swift — but such things do not happen very often. Sometimes young children witness a younger sibling die not long after birth. Experiencing this, the children probably do not feel too strongly about it. Even if the feeling is strong at first, after a while it fades and is forgotten, since "I" still exists and that still feels permanent.

The Buddha once asked his disciples, "What is life?" The disciples had different opinions. Finally one of them said, "Life is between breaths." The Buddha praised him for having such wisdom. This is because after taking a breath in, many people simply die without letting the breath out. When we breathe in, the body tenses up. Breathing out does not take as much effort. This is why practicing the method of counting breaths has its benefit. If practicing well, when one leaves this body without exhaling that last breath, at least that person is in a state of tranquility. Some people are not able to comprehend easily why life is between breaths because they cannot even find their breath. As practice progresses, however, one can slowly feel the breath, and know what a breath is. Furthermore, one will know inhalation and exhalation as a process of arising and ceasing and that the process goes from coarse to subtle.

There are two functions in the practice of stilling and contemplation. One is to settle the mind and enter samadhi. Another is to observe the breath and, from observing inhaling and exhaling, see the phenomenon of arising and ceasing and realize impermanence. When feeling drowsy, you may observe the changes in the breathing — it is slow in and slow out. Sometimes you can notice that the inhaling is longer and exhaling is shorter; at other times it is reversed. This change in pattern is a phenomenon of impermanence.

There are different levels of observing arising and ceasing and realizing impermanence in changes of worldly phenomena. We need to have a basic understanding of the doctrine so that in contemplation we can examine phenomena based on what we have understood. This will also bring us closer to the truth when we go into the subtler aspects of contemplation.

Impermanence in Buddhist doctrine is often viewed as a pessimistic outlook on life. Actually, impermanence or no-self does not have the characteristic of optimism or pessimism. The Buddha explained the phenomena of the world to help us recognize the reality of it. Having understood or realized this true reality, wisdom will manifest. Our own vows or volition influence our choices in life. For eons in the flow of life, we have developed certain attitudes from negative points of view. Take "life is suffering", for example. As soon as we see or have contact with impermanence, we think of escape or liberation in order to end the cycles of birth and death soon. Because we know it would be endless to continue like this, there is a feeling of being tired or disgusted about it and a wish to free ourselves.

Some people feel that life simply repeats itself. In actuality, from the perspective of impermanence, there is no single thing that is repeated. Even in recalling the same incident from the past, there are stories with different versions. We may forget some episodes or add some new elements to it. Impermanence is like this and it is constantly changing. Events that resemble each other do take place, but the words "similar" and "same" have different meanings. For example, many teachers in school face the same group of students every day. Yet, the emotions of the students are different each day. The same goes for the teachers. If teachers saw things from the perspective of impermanence, they would discover that each day is a whole new day. Not knowing what that day would bring, they would not use the eye of permanence to predict what would happen when entering the classroom of even the most badly behaved group. They may carry a preconceived opinion while walking toward the classroom and may even feel a headache before stepping into the room. But maybe one day, upon entering the classroom, no student shows up and the teacher may feel surprisingly relieved because that means "no class!" Or after entering the classroom, the teacher sees that students are all well behaved and looking at the teacher. The teacher does not know what has happened until the teacher spots the principal of the school sitting in the back of the classroom! We have seen in many cases these "unpredictable" rules in life. It is the same with sitting meditation.

Put down All Burdens

Some people use an unchanged mindset to practice, thinking that if the first sitting period went well, the second period will be the same, if not better. Having clinging or attachment, how is it possible that the next period would be better if they cannot let go of a good sitting experience? During the first period, they practice with single-minded concentration, without intentionally adding anything. Slowly they adjust their body and mind so the sitting goes well. In the second sitting period, they are waiting for the same experience to happen, but most likely they will be disappointed since every sitting period is unique. This is why many people who sit well in the first sitting period usually do not sit well in the second session. One would think that the first period went well so there is no reason for the next session not to be as good. But the "no reason" is unreasonable because if your body gets up and moves in a rough fashion as you leave the Chan hall for the restroom break, the concentration has been lost! Perhaps most of you have experienced that it is not so easy to collect your mind, but losing focus happens very quickly. This is why we should sit with the mentality of impermanence. As long as we practice simply focusing the mind, when causes and conditions ripen, the desirable result will come by itself. Try your best to focus on the method. Do not think about the sitting period that has passed, or have expectations about the next period — all is a process of impermanence. As we understand impermanence intimately in this process and apply the principles to our daily life, we will be able to put down many burdens.

If one often views the world with negativity, it is likely one will feel pessimistic. For instance, it often happens that those whom we encounter frequently are not the people we like. But on the other hand, who knows where those with whom we wish to be friends went — we hardly see them! There are many situations in life like this, and we call it "suffering". Because of suffering, some people think about escaping. If we do not understand impermanence, we may feel that every day we go through the same routine and perform the same tasks. Going to work seems unavoidable, for without working we would not have money to spend. Some work nowadays seems very tedious and boring. And, returning home after work, nothing exciting awaits —

even the dreams at night are the same — life does not seem interesting. It is as though each day is repeating itself and it feels tiring.

Practicing with a mood of disenchantment, some people may be able to easily let go of clinging and attachments. Some practitioners practice the method of observing impurity of the body. After a while, they might dislike their body. If at such a time they perceive impermanence, they might desire to quickly end the cyclic fluctuation of suffering. We know that some practitioners keep a distance from society and enter the mountains or deep forest to practice. This may have something to do with the idea of practicing for samadhi or liberation. For the hope of attaining liberation, they are willing to relinquish everything with a thought such as "When one is enlightened and sees the true nature of all dharma, one can even cast off the body, so is there anything else can we not let go of?"

Of all clinging and attachment, the most difficult to let go of is the body. Through meditation, practitioners can reach samadhi and shed desires, relying on only very simple means to maintain life. Commonly, though, we try many things to satisfy our cravings. In addition to things necessary for survival, we want everything to be comfortable. But look at the native dwellers in Malaysia — even though they did not have money, they still managed to live. They knew what is edible and usable in the forest. Their living condition was very simple. Now in civilized society, to some people, even a penny less would seem miserable. We make life so complicated by adding so many things — with only one rag, the native dwellers could wrap their body well, but we cut a whole yard or several yards of cloth into many pieces and then sew them together to make a dress, and some are even annoyed by details such as whether to sew straight or zigzag stitches!

When sitting, some practitioners tend to think about things at home or unfinished work. I often tell retreat participants, "Hang your family affairs outside the door, and do not bring them into the Chan hall." But most people bring them in and, while sitting, they slowly count — not the breath, but the problems at home or work. Indeed, there is too much stuff that burdens the mind. We often seek external objects, wanting to have those things to feel a sense of security. For instance, when going out, some people worry if there is enough money in their wallet. Their mind is always grabbing at things. When they come to practice, they have so many wandering thoughts in their mind that they count wandering thoughts instead of breaths! If we understand this world is impermanent and look back, we find that lots of things we grab at are unnecessary. Since we view these things with the idea of permanence, thinking they will always be with us, we carry them all along and do not want to put them down.

If we are able to observe the more subtle aspects of impermanence, we know that all is in a process of constant change and we will not be so attached to those visible, touchable, and observable things. Such subtle reality is not seen by physical eyes but by the eye of wisdom. Seeing the process of impermanent movements is itself seeing with the eye of wisdom. This requires examination of phenomena, study of Buddhadharma, and then verification through the experience of phenomena, or vice versa. For example, from breathing we can see that life truly is between breaths — a single inhale without an exhale , and life is gone! If we observe carefully, we will discover that every breath is different, that it changes constantly.

We mentioned earlier that, in Burma, there is a method of practice using contemplation of the elements of earth, water, fire, and wind. It is a very detailed and subtle technique. However, observation that has only the function of awareness is not enough for Chan practice — by observing constant changes, we must truly perceive impermanence and no-self. It is the same with observing thoughts. In the beginning, we see coarse thoughts. Slowly we see that they are changing. Even if we do not control the movement of our thoughts, we can notice that they are changing all the time. We are not trying to observe the content of thoughts but only the process of their operation — the arising and ceasing. For example, a moment ago you were thinking of something. A few seconds later, you are thinking of something else. Very rapidly thoughts arise and cease — one thought barely finishes and another one emerges immediately. From this you can actually understand impermanence as well as birth and death.

Sometimes analysis can be useful. For instance, you recall something from the past that made you unhappy. If you can look at it from the perspective of impermanence, you will see that the causes and conditions of that incident have passed and you cannot go back and change what has happened. So you can let it go. If you make it permanent, when images from the memory appear, your emotions will be stirred up and you may feel irritated. However, whatever happened was due to the combination of various factors. If you try to trace them, there are many reasons before this incident that you could investigate and it would be endless. The experience of emotion in this particular incident was because of the mixture of reasons at that particular time. That moment is now over, so the emotion from that moment is also history. If you look at it from your current situation and believe it can be changed, your emotions will probably be stirred up one more time. Then your mind has gone to the past. Also in the process, unpleasant emotions can get aggravated and the memory of it can make you feel increasingly annoyed. In the past, you were unable to see the situation clearly, but now you can see the whole situation clearly. If you think, "It was like this and this; it should have been such and such", you are adding more thoughts to the past confusion. This is a common habit. Having brought the past to the present, thinking that it has not vanished, you continue to drive it and it causes continued suffering.

In seated meditation, when such thoughts arise, if we reflect on them from the perspective of impermanence, they can be let go. By recognizing our emotions and knowing that such emotions are unnecessary, we use the power of self-mastery to bring them to settle. If we can do this, we can let go of many things. What happened in the past can be dealt with using this approach. What is happening at the moment now can also be handled this way. If we can realize impermanence, seeing more subtle movements of the arising and ceasing of the breath, we will know — even as it is happening — that it is the same dynamic.

When things bother us, often we feel uneasy about what has happened. Such problems get worse and worse and life becomes harder and harder, being disturbed day after day. This happens similarly in the Chan hall. Many people cannot let go of family matters, which have obviously passed, and they let them cook again. There is an idiom saying, "Let rising and ceasing be; extinction is happiness". With such an attitude, let what arises cease by itself, and do not let it rise again if it has ceased, regardless of whether it is pleasant or not. This will save you a lot of suffering. We need to understand the principles of Dharma through the process of contemplation, slowly turn the understanding to wisdom, and apply it in daily life. If we let the teaching remain only words that float on the surface, there is no way for us to use it effectively and benefit from it.

When we contemplate impermanence and no-self, the purpose is not to see something but to understand the operation of life through impermanence and no-self. Having comprehended such principles of Dharma, we will be able to put down much mental baggage and let go of it. The more deeply we feel the suffering of life, the more completely we will let go and be free. At the same time, if we can see that life is not that grey and happiness still exists, we can then live it more meaningfully. When we understand the operation of impermanence and no-self, there will be fewer suffering people around us and we will feel this world is actually pure and clean. The world itself is originally pure and clean. It is our afflictions that pollute it. If we can constantly purify ourselves with the teachings of impermanence and no-self, transformation will take place. Truly, if we can investigate, reflect, and verify this, we will begin to let go of many attachments.

What manifests in life from existing to non-existence, from birth to death, will vanish eventually. Aging and death are the final conclusion of this lifetime. Everyone knows that everybody will die, but we do not know when it will come, neither do we know what it is like after death. To most people, death seems horrible. Many people are afraid of death. Imagining the afterlife as described in some books, they are even more terrified. However, if we understand that each life span will reach its end, we can penetrate and see through birth and death and face it calmly when it comes. Chan practice helps us to face death courageously. When it comes, we can accept death with peace, just like accepting a gift. When someone gives us a gift, that's a great thing, isn't it? Death is such a wonderful gift — accept it, quickly! If we can do so, what else in the world can we not put down? What else that is precious can we not let go of?

However, not only are people afraid of death, they even bargain with tiny little things. If you know everyone will die in the end and there is absolutely nothing you can carry with you when the departure time comes, will you still feel the worth of trivial things? Usually we tend to give up quite a bit, but what we get in return is not even worth mentioning. For example, someone goes shopping. They will go to three or four different places, comparing prices and then buying from the place where the price is the lowest. The price in the first store is three dollars and it seems expensive. The second store costs three and a half, the third costs such and such... By the time they walked to the fourth store, it sells for four dollars. So they go back to the first store for the deal. The entire trip takes two hours and they finally buy that one item. They are happy and feel they have accomplished something. This is how people often live their lives.

If we can view things from the angle of impermanence, we see situations as more relaxed. When many burdens are put down, life will be happier. Life can be simple, really. That you are willing to come and participate in a Chan retreat means you have actually let go of a lot of things. In the retreat, there is nothing much to do, but we are still living a meaningful life. The routine in the Chan hall is so simple. Yet, some people are still quite complex — they bring a lot of stuff and make it troublesome. Those who really know about practice are much more simple. Actually, we can all live with simplicity.

Joyful Discovery

If you can deeply reflect on impermanence, you will have the strength to change in daily life and not let yourself live so miserably. Like now, in retreat, during sitting meditation, just sit joyfully! Joyful when there is leg pain. Joyful when you cannot find your breath. Why should we be joyful when we cannot find our breath? Because we have discovered that our mind is coarse and this discovery is an accomplishment! When we cannot count the breath, we realize that we still do not know how to use the method, and this is also a sort of accomplishment. Only when there is leg pain do we know that our leg is capable of having pain to such an extent. Every single incident can let us have a sense of accomplishment. Are you going to live each day full of joy or with unease and anxiety? Either way is living; which way do you want? When we understand and use the teachings of impermanence and no-self to transform our life, we will be able to live and face life with delight. Life is constantly changing. Each day is a new day that allows us to create it as our aspirations lead us. To a certain degree, we do have some power of mastery, so we can live well every day. Knowing with certainty that things are not worth bargaining for, many things can be dropped. Once we let go, the burden in the mind will be significantly lessened.

With thorough understanding of impermanence and no-self, we can then have a sense of equanimity and not to cling to things. We know causes and conditions are like this – it will come when it should and it will go when it should. If we can view the operation of causes and conditions this way in daily life, we will let those that should come, come; and let those which should go, go. We do not pursue what should not come or chase away what should not go. We live each day with mindfulness. When the person whom you do not like does not leave your house, do not try driving him or her out, but make them happy! Then they will run off simply because they cannot stand your treating them so nicely. On the other hand, since you treated this person like a dear friend, when he or she needs to leave, you may now feel sad thinking, "Why do those who should stay always leave?" You see? It all depends on how you view and treat it. If you know how to adjust your attitude and therefore be transformed, many things can be turned from negative to positive.

The newest aspect of IQ (intelligence quotient) is the energy that turns negative to positive, which is the EQ (emotional intelligence quotient). Our everyday life is the operation of the energy of emotions. If we know how to convert negative energy to positive energy, it is "transforming affliction into Bodhi". Only from affliction do we know there is Bodhi, the mind of enlightenment. When we turn affliction to Bodhi, and perceive things from the positive angle instead of the negative, we can live joyfully. Gain or loss to us is merely a process of arising and ceasing in form. Everything is an impermanent phenomenon. If one is desireless, life can be lived happily and with ease. Regardless of whether we are joyful or in pain, the earth still turns each day and the sun still rises every morning. The sun is compassionate – it does not withdraw itself because someone is unhappy.

Sometimes we will face more serious challenges and trials, such as natural disasters and dramatic human accidents. When facing these, only the trained mind is able to quickly transform the conditions; practice cultivates such training. A mind not cultivated can take a long time to adjust to external situations. Without the ability to transform, people may collapse. Every time after a disaster, some people collapse while many other people spring up. For example, after a big earthquake, some people whose own house collapsed might hurry to help clear wreckage of other homes. They are grateful that they are still alive and realize it is only the house that falls, so they can change their mood to go and help other people. But some others, seeing the house fall, might cry non-stop. Would the house be restored immediately because they cried? The mind space differs from person to person, so people do not handle things in the same way. As long as one knows how to work with it, negative energy can quickly be turned to positive energy and one will know what to do at the present moment. The house collapsed; it is useless to cry, and it is better to do something more constructive that can help the situation. For example, your valuables are buried in the collapsed house and you are waiting for the rescue teams to dig. It may take three days and nights but that does not really matter. On the other hand, saving a life cannot wait for another day. If someone is buried in the house, they must be rescued immediately. As long as you know the concept of this kind of transformation, you are one with wisdom, and the entire situation will be utterly different. However, we are merely talking like soldiers fighting a battle on paper — without facing real circumstances we do not know if we have the ability to handle it. Thus we must keep training and continue to practice.

We can elevate our mind with the teachings of impermanence and no-self. Making some changes or adjustments in our views, our attitude will be different. For example, this term of life will end. If we go to sleep and do not wake up, it is not bad at all. What we fear is that it suddenly ends before we have had time to prepare ourselves. To be prepared, in addition to continuously cultivating our mind and raising our awareness by making adjustments, we should do many wholesome deeds in daily life. If we are ready, we can depart at any time. It is the best to go without going back to samsara again. If we can let go of the very last thought at the moment of death, it is liberation. Thus we need to adjust our mind and our life often, carefully observe, and reflect. If we can practice like this over a long period of time, when things happen, the right view of impermanence and no-self will function as needed. When wisdom functions, we can handle things with improvement or perfection.

II

Teachings in
Fourteen-day
Advanced Retreat

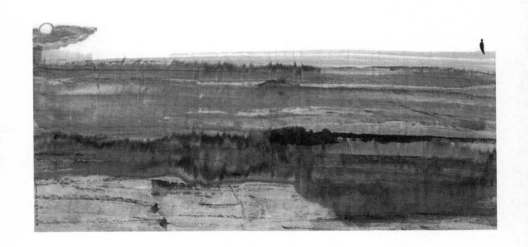

1

The Company of Wandering Thoughts

During seated meditation, the first problem we encounter is interruptions from wandering thoughts. While some of these thoughts are well organized, most of them are random and unorganized and therefore directly interfere with our practice. However, it is not really the wandering thoughts that are disturbing us —they become impediments because we consider them bothersome. Wandering thoughts are actually communicating lots of information to us, and it is up to us how we receive, absorb, and understand them. Facing wandering thoughts helps us to be aware of our problems including our unwholesome attitudes. Once we see with clarity and know the causes of the problems, we can make adjustments and corrections. Thus, do not be afraid of wandering thoughts.

Seeing without Chasing

In daily life some thoughts may delight us. When we think of the events we enjoy and the people we love, we do not feel these thoughts to be bothersome. But what happens when the thoughts are not about what we like? The feeling of aversion or hatred arises and the thoughts are seen as interferences. Sometimes the feeling of anger can allow us to vent a bit since in real life we may be feeling utterly helpless without any alternative way to deal with certain people. At least if we "encounter" them internally in our thoughts, we will not feel troubled but instead feel a relief of some pressure, and we gain a little bit of balance. Viewed from this angle, wandering thoughts seem to have some benefits.

However, if there are many wandering thoughts in everyday life and we yield and follow their lead, we allow them to continue running their course. Sometimes we give them a push by putting our energy on them. Having become accustomed to them, perhaps we do not feel they are bothersome, but why are they such a disruption to us during meditation? It is because when we wish to focus on the method, they pull our attention away without our consent, so we feel restless. If we pay attention to wandering thoughts, we will find that they are reflections of our life. They are our habits or things we ponder over constantly. In recalling the past, either we feel happiness because the memories are sweet, or we feel endless annoyance, regretting the mistakes we made in the past and imagining that things could have turned out better "if only I did such and such..." These imagined scenarios never happen since the causes and conditions of that event have passed, and it is impossible to go back in time. Nonetheless, this endless imagining brings feelings of irritation.

We must face these wandering thoughts when they appear for there is no way we can stop them from coming. When a thought arises and makes us unable to collect our mind inwardly, it does not hurt to try and relax a little bit. Watching it may let us discover that these are just some conditions of our life situation or the opinions that we often circulate within. Having done observation like this, although we know the energy of these wandering thoughts is strong and tends to grab our attention from the method we practice, still, we should simply ignore them and do our best to return to the method. This is because the thought of chasing away wandering thoughts is also a wandering thought, which is actually anger. This happens when we strive to practice with diligence in sitting meditation, but slowly it will pass. If you are able to adopt and can focus on the method, let it sink and go to deep layers within.

As practice goes deeper inward, at each stage wandering thoughts keep us company. Actually, even when we are able to do well with the method, wandering thoughts never leave us — it is only that the coarser ones are put down temporarily and more subtle ones surface. Sometimes, applying the method seems impossible because of the activities of wandering thoughts. Regardless, during sitting, when you notice that coarse wandering thoughts float up, do not try to chase them away, just simply ignore them and hold onto your method. Slowly they will become indistinct and fade away. As keeping on the method reaches a certain stability, the condition of your mind will be adjusted, and practice will enter a subtler state. If you observe carefully when new waves of wandering thoughts surface, you will find that the thoughts that appeared in the beginning of the practice and the thoughts that appear now are different in nature — the former are coarse and the latter are subtler. As they emerge, each layer of wandering thoughts may pull your attention away because by the time you notice it, your mind has already followed it. Nonetheless, as soon as you catch your mind being distracted, bring it back and continue to focus on the method.

Calm-abiding

You may start your practice with the method of counting breaths first. When this becomes stable, put down the counting. This is referred as "realized breath counting". At the beginning, counting is often interrupted. But after you have "realized" counting, this will not happen because your mind has been securely fastened to the counting. As you find the counting becomes too coarse, you can start to practice following the breath. If during this practice your mind is being pulled away, then go back to counting. From being vivid to becoming a blur, wandering thought will slowly fade away as if they are no longer present. In fact, they are still in operation; but because your mind has been trained and adjusted to settle in a subtler state, your reactions to the coarse thoughts are diminished, if not completely unaffected. Having established this solid ground, progress to following the breath again. After some time of sustaining steady following, then settle in this state, which is the so-called "realized breath following". After that, you may take up the method of "calm-abiding" (shamatha in Sanskrit).

In the beginning of practicing the method of calm-abiding, it is common that people do not know where the so-called "still point" is located. Or, you may have an idea about it but your mind seems vacant and clings to some external objects or conditions. Even though following the breath is subtler as an approach of practice, there is still the breath to focus on; but in calm-abiding practice, this is all gone. Sometimes even the tactile sensation is gone and only mental images are left. At times when it can feel empty-minded or void, the impulse to grab at something will surge. After sensing the breath is still there, you return to following the breath. After awhile, your mind enters stillness again. Or in some cases when wandering thoughts become coarse, you return to counting. When you can again follow the breath, then your mind goes back to stillness. By the time stillness is achieved, you are able to settle on the method. Even though there is awareness of the wandering thoughts, your mind is unaffected by them. This is a samadhi state in the realm of form.

If this state can be sustained without deliberate effort, simply stay with it. Gradually it will enter deep meditative absorption. However, wandering thoughts will still accompany this process. Because concentration has gone sufficiently deep and the mind is settled and steady, the thoughts that surface now will be things that are deeply hidden or afflictions that are subtler in manifestation. If wandering thoughts were about what happened recently, it means they are coarse, and the practice is also on the surface. When practice is solid, wandering thoughts will be in harmony with the wholesome Dharma; otherwise your mind is easily sidetracked. Continue to steadily apply the method even though your mind may experience ups and downs in the process. Eventually when your mind is settled on one object, cultivation of stillness begins. After the state of stillness is reached, contemplation will be the next phase of practice, or one has entered a deeper state of samadhi.

The Danger of Arrogance

Perhaps there are practitioners who wish to gain some super-knowledge or special ability through meditation. In other words, in a state of samadhi, the strength of mind will immensely increase, and in such conditions, without wisdom as guidance, one can be controlled by some sort of superpower and eventually be led astray. It is like having weapons in hand without ethical discipline — the weapons become a tool for producing evil karma. This is why, without the guidance of right views, before cultivating meditative absorption, such hazards are prone to happen.

Sometimes such a problem is not only a matter of right knowledge but also an issue of mentality. We often remind practitioners to keep a simple mind in meditation because, if the method works well, one can enter a state of dhyana; and in the state of dhyana, contemplation will awaken the wisdom within. You all know these concepts and ideas, but when you sit, your mind does not listen to you. This is why some people become more and more sidetracked as they practice meditation – it is because the subtle aspects of mind are not adjusted to be in accord with right views of the Dharma.

Among the factors hindering practice, the most common one is the mindset of arrogance. Once arrogance arises, a variety of problems will follow intimately. For instance, the meditators compare themselves with others. If others sit well, they feel inadequate. If others do not sit well, they want to show off their capability. If practicing the method is going well for them, arrogance grows. If they do not win the imagined competition in their head, they become jealous. When jealousy arises, they want to use phony ability to inflate and decorate themselves, making small progress appear big, worrying that others do not notice their practice. Or, if the person on the neighboring seat is sitting well, they attempt to disturb their fellow practitioner to make them lose concentration and "fail". Do not think that every thought which passes through your mind is wholesome – all sorts of tricks can be fabricated by a mind filled with jealousy.

Wandering thoughts themselves are present as reflections of the conditions of our daily life. The habits of daily life are deeply ingrained in our mind and become wandering thoughts in meditation. If in life you react with jealousy when others are better than you, the likelihood is that you will behave the same on the sitting cushion. Mentality is a very subtle thing. If we let a harmful mindset succeed due to our neglect, the consequences can be enormous. It will be too late to remember to correct our mind because the thoughts of arrogance, jealousy, or inadequacy may be too overwhelming and powerful and may cover all of our wholesome thoughts. Then the method is lost and practice does make any progress. The more our practice fails to make progress, the more this mind of arrogance cannot stand other people's success.

Sooner or later it will lead practice in a wrong direction.

The above-mentioned situations show that one's meditation has not yet entered the stage of samadhi. If it had, the danger would be even more serious due to the power of samadhi. If this is the case, after a seven-day retreat, not only are the methods of practice not adopted at all, but one has also made oneself miserable. If this type of subtle mindset is not adjusted at the outset, not only can one not practice with vigilance, but also one can stumble and regress. Hence, we really must pay close attention to our wandering thoughts, particularly regarding arrogance.

There can be cases in which arrogance arises and encourages meditators to exert more effort. This happens usually for those persons who have strong will and determination. If you sit continuously for two sitting periods, they might sit for three periods to show you their capability. Even when the leg pain is so unbearable that their whole body sweats with chill, they still pretend and stay on the cushion simply to demonstrate their strength. Is that really a diligent practice?

There is an example of extreme arrogance in the history of Buddhism — that example being Devadatta. Suffering from the poison of arrogance, Devadatta created lots of bad karma. For instance, he purposefully advocated ascetic rules that the Buddha did not set out as disciplines for practice, such as abstaining from eating fish or salt. He did so in order to attract the Buddha's newer disciples who were unfamiliar with the genuine Dharma, so that he could gather them together and form his own sangha or congregation. He also convinced a prince to take over his father's throne, the king of Magadha, because if he were successful, Devadatta himself could become the new Buddha. In addition to being very handsome — while the Buddha had thirty-two auspicious aspects, Devadatta had thirty — Devedatta was a cousin of the Buddha, the brother of Ananda, and also one of the Shakya clan. His jealousy and arrogance together made him generate very bad karma. Imagine it — did not Devadatta have a deep practice or knowledge of the Dharma? It was said that he could recite a few hundred thousand of the Buddha's verses! Nonetheless, his practice had a serious problem because the deep afflictions were not rooted out.

All of us have the potential of having such problems. This is why we must pay attention to our mental state in practice. Sometimes just a fleeting distraction can take us in a wrong direction, like arrogance did with Devadatta. It is of paramount importance that we guard and manage the tendency of arrogance in practice. Arrogance is one of the cardinal afflictions. It makes people compulsively compete with others in almost everything. It is extremely important to pay attention to our own psychological conditions; this type of mindset needs to be disciplined and adjusted.

Remind yourself often about this — practice is an individual affair, not something to be compared with others. In practice there is no number ranking such as number one or number two. Some worldly gains may be obtained by unlawful means, but it is absolutely impossible in spiritual practice. Practice is to open our own mind and take a good look at it. The more sincere you are with your mind, the better you can implement the methods. If you add something impure to it, it is difficult to practice, because practice is the inwardly oriented cultivation of mind, not the pursuit of anything outward. If you sense such a mindset in your sitting, remind yourself constantly to correct it immediately. Then, your right knowledge and right view will be able to function and take you in the right direction and to the right destination. Do not be anxious because of the appearance of wandering thoughts and afflictions. From them we can truly see the issues we need to deal with in practice.

2

Managing the Mind Environment

Some people feel that they cannot participate in Chan retreats or practice at home, either because of time and space constraints or interference from external conditions. However, the biggest interference does not come from outside but from within. If annoyance does not arise internally due to our afflictions, there will be ways to practice under any circumstances. The source of the problem lies in the inner environment of our mind. At some phases of practice, the impact of subtle affliction and deluded thoughts can be great. Thus avoidance is not an option and we must understand and manage the condition of our mind with great clarity.

Accepting with Objectivity

Generally we do not like to face our unwholesome behavior in daily life and see exactly how it has happened. Often people's attitude towards affliction is "better not to touch it." Some people disguise it by using wholesome deeds such as making donations to charities. When the action of giving is mixed with impure motivations, there might be thoughts of gaining something in return for charitable donations or for fame and publicity. If these thoughts are not very strong in a person's mind, it will not become a serious impediment. But over time these thoughts can become karma and retribution with the potential to reincarnate. Even if they received something good in return for a charitable donation, it is still within the cyclic flow of samsara. It is not entirely rare to see people make generous offerings, but the action is a mixture of wholesome and unwholesome motivations.

Many participants behave the same way in Chan retreats when they are motivated by the pursuit of some meditative states. Once they gain some pleasant feelings, they think their practice has "gotten somewhere. " Their mind is filled with deluded thoughts but they do not want to face them. Even when they talk about it, they try to avoid mentioning their afflicted conditions. Sometimes they are not even willing to discuss it in individual interviews or they will touch on it only briefly, thinking that, by ignoring it, their problem has vanished. Such afflictions, remaining in the mind, will become obstacles in practice. There are many unbeneficial mindsets that may float up during practice which we may try to avoid by going around them. However, we will be turning and turning in the same spot unable to escape them. If we do not ferret them out, it is impossible to see them clearly.

Avoiding or pretending that they do not exist is one common attitude towards deluded thoughts and afflictions. Another is exaggeration. When we are unable to do something, we think it is due to our heavy karma. For instance, when some people wish to practice and the family is unsupportive, they think of it as an issue of very heavy karma. Actually, it is not the heavy karma "outside" but most of the time it is the barrier within a person's own mind. It is not an impediment of karma but is an impediment of their affliction. Yes, karma can become an obstruction; but if you do not see it as an obstruction, it is not. Difficult situations are not necessarily bad. As a matter of fact, many people practice under unfavorable conditions. In such cases, "bad karma" is not a hindrance but, in fact, can be turned into favorable conditions.

To some people, good conditions may become a hindrance. Why? If they live very comfortably at home, for instance, when they think of the possible leg pain that might arise in sitting meditation, they become afraid to come to a retreat and participate. If they take things for granted and do not properly take advantage of the opportunities provided by their favorable environment, the favorable conditions can be a hindrance — it blocks their practice.

We need to understand that both affliction and wholesome thought are functions of mind, and they are also energy — affliction is negative energy and wholesome thought is positive energy. The teaching that "affliction is itself bodhi" means precisely that negative energy can be transformed into positive energy.

We know that everyone has emotions. Because we often make emotion a negative energy, it causes us to handle our daily life not so intelligently or "with low EQ" (emotional intelligence), as people say nowadays. If we can see clearly that emotions fluctuate and can transform negative energy into positive energy, the function of emotions can be more desirable. For instance, do not avoid facing your anger when someone criticizes you. Why? Because the emotion of anger indicates that we are normal human beings. If one is not angry after being admonished, it is perhaps for one of the following reasons: this person is a saint, or an idiot, or dead. We are ordinary and normal people. When being scolded, of course the emotions will come out. If we let the negative energy clash with the other person, it is likely to cause conflict. However, if we let the other person know that we are angry, there are ways for the emotion to be transformed.

Probably a mother often encounters such situations. After being scolded, the child says, "Mom, are you angry?" Then you will be unable to continue being angry. Why? Because the child informed you about your emotion — the child is helping you to transform your anger. You hear it and might think, "Why am I angry? Is it for the good of my child or just venting my frustrations?" Looking within, you can make an adjustment. You might tell yourself while being angry, "Angry... angry... angry... put it down! Put it down! Put it down!" In this way, being aware of your agitation can be helpful. It is similar to hearing noise — try not to discriminate but simply repeat, "I am aware. I am aware. I am aware. Put it down. Put it down. Put it down." Then return to the method. The sound will no longer bother you.

Handling by Transformation

Affliction and wandering thoughts flow with us all the time. It is impossible to escape from them. However, they are not as terrible as we imagine. Many people speak about them as if they are terrible and imagine that the three poisons of greed, anger, and delusion will kill the life of wisdom. In fact, being transformed to non-greed, non-anger, and non-delusion, they become "bodhi" — the mind of enlightenment. This is wholesome dharma.

When a feeling of suffering from greed, anger, or delusion appears with wandering thoughts, if you do not know how to deal with it at the moment, put it down temporarily and do not let yourself be bothered by it. This is the method of calm-abiding meditation. These thoughts may continue to churn and only the coarse ones are put down. If we relax the body and mind every day and clear those coarse thoughts, they will not accumulate. Similarly, if we can clear up the stress and problems we face during the day through sitting meditation or other ways, we will not carry them to our sleep and they will not stack up as tomorrow's poison, and the space of our mind will be vast.

We are constantly accumulating problems, from small deluded thoughts to big ones. If we let the root of deluded thoughts grow deep, once it has clutched our mind, the cleanup job is difficult. The method of calm-abiding that we employ is to first cleanse coarse wandering thoughts. Those subtle ones can then be rooted out through contemplation.

During the retreat, as your mind adjusts to a more subtle condition, you will see subtle afflictions. Although subtle, the impact is not necessarily weak because they stick in our mind very deeply and tightly. So after some coarse wandering thoughts have passed, the deep and subtle wandering thoughts will surface. Their power of interference can be quite strong. Even if we ignore them and continue to work with the method, they still come to light from time to time. This is because we had only avoided them before and had not really removed the source. What to do in such situations? Just continue to sit and try your best to return to the method. Slowly they will subside. These are deep-rooted wandering thoughts. We had only trimmed the branches or part of the trunk a little bit, but the root is still there. After a while they will grow out again and continue to interfere. This is the reason why we must continue the practice of contemplation, using wisdom to eliminate them from the root. This requires a long-term commitment to practice.

When we contemplate, we must be based in the Buddhadharma. As wandering thoughts arise, look into them with the teaching of impermanence and no-self. This requires strength in the mind. Alternatively, one can view wandering thoughts from a different angle, which is to view them as normal. After seeing this clearly, these can be transformed. This not only prevents wandering thoughts from becoming affliction but also turns them into a supreme supportive condition.

Viewing life from the aspect of transformation, we know that living in this world, we cannot avoid people; clinging and attachment to them makes us bound and not liberated. However, we can change this narrow sense of love to great compassion and treat people with compassion instead of being attached to them. For example, we love our parents. What we can do is to consider all elders of similar age as our parents, then attachment can be transformed into a positive energy. The mind of compassion is wishing them to be happy and free from suffering. Loving them is to wish them happiness without suffering. When we express this with actions, it becomes wholesome energy instead of clinging. However, first we must see the operation of wandering thoughts clearly. Only then will we be able to make transformation happen.

This kind of transformation has been exhibited by many masters in the school of Chan. Some masters have distinct personalities as a result of accumulated habits. They might not eliminate all of their habits but rather transform them into expedient means for delivering sentient beings, since certain personality traits are more suitable for helping people with similar personality traits. Actually, habits themselves are not good or bad; they are only a tendency cultivated over a long time. If this tendency is in accord with affliction, it becomes a harmful habit. If it is in accord with the wisdom of Dharma, it can be utilized to deliver sentient beings. As the proverb says, "Like attracts like." People whose karma is similar tend to draw together.

At the time of the Buddha, after the Buddha finished a discourse, his newly ordained monks would sit around their admired idols — the senior disciples — and ask them for teachings of the Dharma. Those monks who preferred ascetic practice would go to Mahākasyapa while those who enjoyed discussions would go to Mahākatyāyana, and those who delighted in wisdom practices would go to Shariputra. The Buddha was an open-minded enlightened being. That is why after the Buddha's parinirvana, sectarian Buddhism among his disciples was a common phenomenon. Actually, when the Buddha was still alive, there was already separation among some disciples. True democratic society is like this. The Buddha did not consider such as a problem or worry about disunion of his disciples. The senior disciples had their own strength or area of expertise, which were inherited from their personalities. Therefore in the development of the Chan School in later eras, there emerged several sects and each had its special character such as "the stick of Master De-Shan" or "the shout of Master Lin-ji."

Managing with Understanding

After seeing wandering thoughts clearly, our practice is to transform, cleanse and eliminate those that can be eliminated. This is a rather long process. If not handled properly, deluded thinking will hinder practice. Do not fear that wandering thoughts will come out. If we practice with diligence, we should be able to handle them instead of feeling helpless. It is just that sometimes we are unwilling to take a good look at them. However, in the process, only if we know how to handle our problems can we gradually make progress. We can improve our mind conditions by observing wandering thoughts and employing right views and methods.

The method to clear those wandering thoughts that come as soon as you sit down on the cushion is to ignore them. Simply abide in your method until they fall away since these are coarse and obvious afflictions on the surface of consciousness. As long as you put them down, they will pass. When subtler afflictions appear, you need to carefully observe. If you have a fairly good understanding of the doctrine of the Buddhadharma, you may directly apply the teachings of emptiness or no-self in contemplation. In other words, you penetrate the true nature of all phenomena and cut off delusion at the root. This is the most ideal.

It is fine if you do not yet have such ability to contemplate; simply observe the afflictions. Afflictions reflect our daily life, personality and various phenomena in our mind, and they are definitely related to us. Even if the thoughts are about others, in the end, you will find that the leading character in the story is "us" because it is we who caused these troubles, so naturally they will bounce back to us. Others are not at all the problem.

Sometimes when we sit, it feels almost like being in a dream — the body and mind are forgotten. When wandering thoughts arise, in the beginning, some of them may not be what we have experienced in life events. However, eventually we find the main character to be ourselves. It is the same during dreams — no matter how the story of the dream develops, the key person is "me," because the self is the dream maker.

Sometimes you find that your sitting is in a drowsy but not completely drowsy condition. This is the case when our mind is relatively concentrated but when we have lost awareness of the body. At such times, if wandering thoughts are strong, they will obstruct our awareness, and our whole body and mind will follow them. Then when the gong is struck by the timekeeper at the end of the sitting period, we realize we are sitting in the Chan hall and feeling as if we had just been in a dream. This does not indicate real drowsiness. Real drowsiness is entering a state of stupor where you are completely asleep and even snore. At that time, there will be dreams. When the sound of gong wakes you up, you will feel very tired. Both conditions are similar in that the awareness is lost, but the latter is due to the body being exhausted. One holds the body erect and then enters sleep, not knowing what one is doing. Even if you nod and wake up suddenly, you will continue to fall asleep. Sometimes the method is working, but the mind sinks into an unaware state, and wandering thoughts are still there. If you are not even aware of the wandering thoughts, be careful — to continue like this you will fall into unconsciousness — it is not entering samadhi, in which all thoughts have ceased.

Such a dream-like condition in meditation indicates that wandering thoughts are subtle or past experience is deeply hidden. If the memory is still there after waking up, it does not hurt to investigate it and recall what might have happened. Maybe it is about something within present memory or maybe it has happened in dreams. It can also be that, after an experience has passed, it only leaves a shallow impression until someday something happens that one feels is familiar but cannot remember when it happened — it could be that it had appeared in the image of wandering thoughts.

Looking at Consciousness

When the first five bodily sense faculties stop functioning and the mind inwardly collects, many hidden images from consciousness may appear. From the viewpoint of the Consciousness-Only School, this is manifestation of the seeds stored in consciousness, the eighth consciousness (ālaya-vijñāna). Often only at such times can the sixth consciousness and the eighth consciousness connect. Because it is passing through the seventh consciousness (manas), the central figure of the images must be the self. This is saying that after the seventh consciousness, all functions become "self." Thus, regardless of how the dream situation evolves, it will be around the self.

If, when it is about time for the seeds of karma in the eighth consciousness to manifest, the sixth consciousness is linked to it, and its impact will appear in the sixth consciousness. Having this image in the sixth consciousness, there is an impression, and it will appear in dreams or in sitting meditation. This is because when dreaming, the first five sense faculties completely stop. Such a state can also be reached when sitting meditation goes well and the bodily sense faculties are cast off. When the mind is concentrated and the seeds in the eighth consciousness appear, the sixth consciousness can sense it and will receive the information. Maybe after a few days when the retribution of these karmic seeds manifest, one feels familiarity as if it has happened before. But when one returns to reality and uses coarse consciousness (that can be sensed) to recall that incident, it may seem completely unfamiliar.

Such appearances of hidden things is helpful to our practice. Without them, we will be unaware of their existence. When we go deeply into our mind layer after layer, we will find that wandering thoughts are communicating information to us, and each layer of affliction is telling us something.

When we are approaching the end of our lifetime and certain evil karma has been strongly generated by us, this karma will push us towards the hellish destinies. For example, people who work in the slaughtering business have the heavy karma of killing. Usually, retribution of such karma will manifest before death and they may see where they will enter in the next life. This means that the seeds in the store consciounessness and the karma created in the sixth consciousness have manifested. This is the type of principal or directional karma, which is unchangeable after manifesting in the body of a human and is only changeable after this lifetime has ended. It is the type of karma that is heavy enough to manifest before any change can take place.

When you sit in meditation, you can take a look and see which category of your wandering thoughts is dominant. From that you can really see your afflictions because they are the function of the psyche. In talking about afflictions, many people tend to exaggerate and make them sound like some incurable disease. Actually it is not that severe, only that we feel these afflictons to be huge and corrupt. If this feeling is too overwhelming, our mind will be short of strength and unable to employ the method. Or when we are unable to use the method, we think it is because of the hindrance of karma. To look from a positive viewpoint, wandering thoughts simply reflect our daily life. For example, after creating karma of unwholesome speech or action, these will regress back to our mind. Infused in the consciousness, they then become seeds in the store of consciousness or a hidden habit. When they operate again, we can see them.

If the ability of self-mastery or contemplation is strong, you can use the principle of Buddhadharma to illuminate your mind. You can try to intentionally think of something that made you disturbed in the past and see if you are able to apply the method. At such times, if your practice is going well and stable, those wandering thoughts will quickly dissolve after arising. Why? Because they are too coarse. Your mind is dwelling in a subtle state, such coarse thoughts are unable to stick.

If there are coarse afflictions during sitting and your mind is easily pulled away, it indicates that the method has not been implemented well. But this is okay and there is no need to be anxious. The more anxious you are, the less likely you will be able to adopt the method. Just remind yourself to keep coming back to the method and adjust your mind. Try keeping the awareness focused on the method, and it can overcome the problem. There is no need to fight it. As long as your mind is adjusted into a subtle condition, wandering thoughts will settle down. If you can do this and let each layer of wandering thoughts appear and be ignored, the condition of your mind will adjust and become refined. This is more of an approach of stillness. Then, because of the strength of awareness, you can observe, investigate, and use the method to dissolve wandering thoughts. Slowly affliction will be cut off and the momentum of cyclic flow will end.

During sitting, wandering thoughts will surely appear. It is unavoidable. Hence, we must face them with right attitude — being neither overzealous nor underzealous in handling them — use the approach of the middle way to perceive affliction and wandering thoughts. If they can be transformed, do so, otherwise just put them down. In the end, root out affliction if it can be done.

3

Raising Mindfulness

When wandering thoughts keep coming in meditation, and through those thoughts we see what we cling to from the past, what bothers us is that our diligent practice is disrupted. If frustration constantly arises, there will be emotions of anger. When pleasant memories of the past keep surfacing, there is the arising of greed or more delusion. Thus we try various ways to overcome these obstructions. In fact, what bothers us has happened in daily life; these obstructions appear with wandering thoughts in meditation because usually we have treated them with an attitude of "mental victory" or self-deception, but the problem was not really solved. It is like in the famous Chinese novella of Lu Xun The True Story of Ah Q — the main character Ah Q's personality is weak and, when intimidated by other people, he does not dare to react or confront but would say it to himself, "Today is my unlucky day." Psychologically he sees himself as a winner — Many times when we encounter a setback, we fabricate some story to show that we are the champion and therefore gain some inner balance from it.

Seeing the "I"

In actualilty, all sorts of problems we face in daily life are consequences and retributions of our karmic action. Seen from this vantage point, one would think that we should put these things down. However, not only do we not let them go, we hide them deep in our mind. Then when we do quiet down in practice, naturally they come out in wandering thoughts. With some difficult cases, because of the injustice we feel, we make up stories to mentally balance ourselves. We continue like this and generate karma as well as create similar consequences.

In reality, we cannot be the director of our movies because we do not know what will happen and cannot be prepared. In writing a story, the personality of the main character can be made up. However, the author may find that at certain points of development, the character can no longer be controlled, especially in long novels. In the end, the conclusion may not be at all what the author has imagined.

This is the process of causes and conditions. Because different causes and conditions come into being, the result is not going to be the same as we originally designed. If we let them continue to develop as habit, we will continue to create more causes and conditions and driving forces. If we keep fueling this non-stop, it will be endless. To stop driving this endless cycle, we use the method of calm- abiding to observe it, thus being aware and not letting it arise again. We can also put these problems into categories and investigate and discover their causes. For example, when we face frustration, we can see the weakness in our personality which prevents us from accomplishing things. In this way we can see ourself and the subtler aspects of our affliction more clearly.

Many times we know what to do to resolve issues and make ourselves feel more fulfilled, but due to heavy vexations, what often transpires is the arising of arrogance. This is why sometimes a person would rather be wrong than to make amends. If they did make amends they would consider themselves to be "losing face." There are many situations in daily life where we will see our own weakness if we face it squarely. Maybe we do not have the courage to accept or correct our mistakes, but if we can learn from the lessons of our mistakes, it is possible that when similar things happen again, we will know to transform the negative energy of affliction to the positive energy of compassion. This is what we can learn from observing our wandering thoughts.

Seeing ourselves clearly and improving ourselves is the practice. If you think that one day, after you have sat on the cushion for a long time, something spectacular will happen — that you will be enlightened and suddenly become a different person with all vexations vanished — this is a complete fantasy and utterly impossible. In reality, practice is to continuously improve our personality and rectify our mind. Do not be afraid to dig out your vexations or your wandering thoughts, for only after being exposed can these issues be resolved. Another important attitude is that of sincerely wanting to make changes. Some people see their problems but are unwilling to change their habits, because they have lived like this for many years and others have been accustomed to and accepted them as they are. This stubbornness in the personality is like a solid rock. With such mentality, practice may reach a certain place but will be unlikely to advance much further. Some classic texts describe vexations to be as hard as diamonds that only wisdom can break. This is telling us that in the process of practice, we need to see our vexations and continuously adjust and improve ourselves. Only then, as we see the nature of dharma, can we eliminate our vexations from the root.

Movement of Chi

Sometimes we find that our practice seems difficult to deepen and we circle around and around the same place. This is because we were unable to break through the solid barrier or did not wish to take the leap. For example, some students "play" with the movement of chi or energy flow in their bodies when they sit on the cushion. They feel the chi move here and there and they feel happy or comfortable, but this is not really practicing the method, merely regulating the body. In some cases, instead of being a natural phenomenon, this sort of chi movement becomes a habit.

When we use the method of following the breath, the chi in the body may start to move because with our mind needing to be refined, the body needs to be adjusted accordingly. When the whole body is relaxed, such chi movement might take place. It can be more obvious for those who have physical issues. Chi movement is like an exercise inside the body and can enable one to have pleasant feelings of lightness or bliss. If one indulges in it, rather than enhancing one's practice with it, it will stagnate and become mere physical gymnastics and a hindrance to practice.

This is the reason I do not encourage coming to sitting meditation after learning qigong (a health care system that manages chi) unless one's physical condition is so poor that they have to use it as therapy. After learning qigong exercises, many practitioners have the tendency to cling to body movement and sensations. Why? It is because the physical condition of the body will improve with such exercise, but this is transitional. What we need to learn is to use meditative absorption to cultivate wisdom. Otherwise it will remain as the qigong of body adjustment and, after reaching a certain state of samadhi, these practitioners might stop and completely forget the ultimate aim of Chan practice. Hence, this mentality must be adjusted. When chi movement takes place, let it run its natural course. Sometimes it may be strong and cannot be stopped. Wait until its strength lessens, then slowly adjust and eventually let it pass.

The process of mind regulation is the same. Being aware of afflictions and problems, if you hesitate in letting them go, they will likely surface during sitting meditation. It is like when you keep something in mind and don't let it go, it will likely appear repeatedly in dreams. If you think of these things every time you sit, running with them in circles, this only increases affliction and in a sense, you do not improve at all. Time and time again it will be the same. So in the cultivation of mind, one needs to progress deeper step by step and at the same time, let go step after step.

During sitting meditation we often let the force of wandering thoughts run continuously by steering it. Only when our awareness is very sharp and concentration is strong can we dwell deeply in the mind without driving it further by following its run. We can also try replacing wandering thoughts with mindfulness, for example, of the Buddha and the Dharma.

Mindfulness of the Buddha

Mindfulness of the Buddha is a simple method for practice, which is to keep raising the name of the Buddha in the mind. The name of the Buddha symbolizes the meritorious virtue and wisdom of the Buddha. Reciting the name of the Buddha is to be mindful of that. In the scriptures there are ten verses of praising the Buddha, which help us to recall the virtue and wisdom of the Buddha and further raise the mind of longing and taking refuge in the Buddha. This mindfulness can be used to replace wandering thoughts.

You can take a name of a buddha or bodhisattva who resonates with you as a way of keeping mindfulness. When the condition of your mind becomes quiet and subtle, reciting the name of the Buddha will help it to stick in the mind. Usually when people recite the Buddha's name, their mind is scattered and therefore the name is just one of the wandering thoughts. Even though it is a good thought, it lacks strength so one finds there are still lots of wandering thoughts while reciting the name of the Buddha. When the name is lost in the stream of wandering thoughts, a person is not even aware of it. This is why some people use a mala as an aid to help maintain focus on the name of the Buddha.

We can also use the sense faculty of ear to listen to the recitation of Buddha's name by others, letting it sink into and constantly purify our mind. During retreats in which mindfulness of the Buddha is the method for practice, there is a period of fast-paced recitation before entering stillness, with one name repeatedly recited. This can help strengthen the impression of Buddha's name in consciousness. When it suddenly stops, one feels as if the Buddha's name is still heard in their mind — this is turning the external sound into an internal image. Fast recitation helps to prevent wandering thoughts from jumping in because during recitation, mindfulness is kept on the name of the Buddha.

We can also use the method of counting, such as reciting "Amituofo, one, Amituofo, two," to constantly remind ourselves to keep focused. Recite the number after the name in order to help hold attention on the name. When you find there is only "Amituofo" without the number, it indicates that awareness has been pulled away and your mind did not concentrate. At such times, go back to counting the breath again. Keep practicing for a while, as the names you recite are seamless, wandering thoughts will have no gap to slip in. Once the count can be put down, then you can practice the method with single-mindedness.

At the beginning of this practice, since our mind is easily distracted, we can rely on external sound to hold our attention. When practicing with a group of people, you may recite out loud or listen to the sound of Buddha's name. It is very convenient to do so nowadays because there are recordings to aid us in the practice of recitation. Some day there may be even better ways to assist us due to the development of technology. This is entering meditative practice from the sense faculty of the ear. It is useful because in the beginning of practice we are accustomed to clinging to external objects through the faculty of eye, ear, and body. When the function of awareness becomes strong, we can turn our attention to inner objects.

There are many more ways to practice mindfulness of the Buddha. One example is looking at statues of the Buddha. The statue must be very dignified. Upon seeing it, one is likely to raise the feeling of joy, and the image of the statue can be imprinted in consciousness. When one reaches such a state, even with the eyes closed, the image will appear. This is the type of samadhi mentioned in the Pratyutpanna-samadhi Sutra, wherein the Buddha stands right in front and can be seen clearly. It is a deep state of practice. However if you just stay in that state, it is not wisdom, and you need to practice further. You can use this method for cultivating samadhi, which is to transform external objects of the eye slowly into an internal image.

The above-mentioned methods are all about utilizing mindfulness to recite the name of the Buddha. As mindfulness is strengthened, the illusory or demonic wandering thoughts or afflictions will gradually diminish because mindfulness is being concentrated and becoming powerful. In daily life, as mindfulness becomes the central stream of thoughts on which our thinking and ideals are based, the afflictions will also lessen.

Contemplation on the Dharma

The practice of mindfulness of the Dharma is a little more complicated since Buddhadharma encompasses various methods of contemplation. Some of these are for counteracting wandering thoughts and afflictions. For example, contemplating impurity of the body uses the form of the body as the object of contemplation. Sometimes practitioners even go to see corpses. They then gradually turn this external object into the form of oneself. When they enter meditative absorption, they can see their own body decaying and bloody with insects crawling all over , etc. This is mainly for counteracting desire and greed. If one is deeply attached to the body, this method can be effective.

However, this method has drawbacks, and sometimes the application of it can cause a problem. It is as if one has a certain disease and uses a medicine to cure it. When the sickness is gone, there is no need to continue taking the medicine. And if the effect of the medicine is still strong, it can cause the condition of another illness. Thus after reaching a certain state, it is necessary to adjust the use of this method. For example, in observing the bones of the dead, instead of contemplating their breakdown, one may contemplate purity of white bones. This can have a balancing effect.

In order for this practice to be effective, it is best to first settle your mind. If you cannot concentrate while seeing the body decaying, there may be more than one reason. On one hand it may cause fear; on the other hand, it may cause a feeling of disgust or resistance to the body. With such conditions, you will not be able to penetrate in contemplation. Hence, one must take the attitude of "neutral" in doing this practice. When the mind is able to collect itself and be stable, use the eye faculty to observe, reflect, and from there, to contemplate impurity. This is a type of contemplation by visualization. Using this method to contemplate one's parents or loved ones with the vision of their being happy can be helpful in raising the mind of compassion.

The practice of contemplation is to use methods from the teachings of the Buddhadharma to strengthen the power of concentration. When concentration is strong enough to enable steady mindfulness, the arising of wandering thoughts or afflictions will slowly diminish and their power will also lessen. From the beginning of practice to reaching such a state of balance, there are sequential steps to follow as in a system of practice. These steps can assist us in letting go of attachment to the body and all sorts of worldly desires, as well as raising the thought of emancipation or liberation.

The most important contemplation is on the Dharma of causes and conditions. To someone who lacks wisdom and is unclear about situations, it is a very useful antidote. From the wandering thoughts we can see causes and conditions. Often we do not see them because we tend to run away and are afraid of looking at them. If we really face them, we will find that all wandering thoughts have their causes and conditions as well as karma and retribution. This perception helps us to establish right understanding about causes and conditions.

The Dharma teaches us the right views of good and evil, karma and retribution, the cyclic fluctuation of the three periods of past, present, and future. These principles can be seen in our wandering thoughts. We can also investigate the real content of wandering thoughts through study of the doctrines. This is contemplating causes and conditions. In contemplating dependent origination, it actually helps us to constantly adjust our views and concepts in order to perceive life with a right outlook. Understanding this principle helps us to know how to approach it if we want to change and improve ourselves.

So after reaching a certain stage in practice and seeing our own weaknesses and vexations, if we want to make adjustments we can create the causes and conditions for change. In the beginning, the process of change might be slow, or the effect might not be obvious. As it continues to strengthen, the impact of adjustment in our mind will be manifested in daily life. If adjustments take place in our mind, this itself reflects the causes and conditions, and also dependent origination. However, this type of contemplation is on immediate phenomena – there is still a need for understanding the theory or doctrine as a solid foundation.

To contemplate wandering thoughts is to verify the theory through wandering thoughts, or investigate wandering thoughts according to the theory in order to know what is correct. If this practice of contemplation can deepen continuously and we are able to make adjustment in ourselves, confidence about the Dharma of causes and conditions will be stronger and our actions will also be improved accordingly. Wisdom will then arise from the contemplation of dependent origination and the functions of wisdom will manifest.

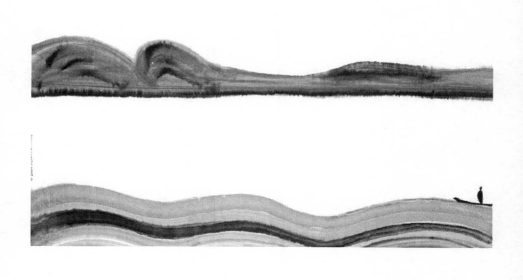

4

Causes and Effects

When cultivation of mind has reached a certain stage, the phenomenon of causality will manifest. It is not telling us that we won a victory. In the operation of cause and effect, there is no such thing as winners or losers, only the result of causes and conditions that meet and manifest. Sometimes when enountering mistreatment or injustice in daily life, we realize that such a mental condition is not going in the direction of Chan practice. If we truly face ourselves and understand that the afflicting actions of others may be due to a lack of knowledge of cause and effect, but we know that our own actions are in accord with the principle of causality and that our ultimate aim is liberation, then we can adjust our mentality. The consequences of karma that others have created will be borne by others, and what we have created will be borne by ourselves. All phenomena are in the movement of causes and conditions, not only in the material world but also in our body and mind. If the direction of practice is correct and one's actions are based on the Dharma, one can go straight ahead on the path.

Believing in Causality

A slight affliction in our mind can generate the flow of causes and conditions; a clear mind will lead us to the path of liberation. Do we want our mind to be purified, or to continue to fluctuate with afflictions in samsara? Through contemplation, we can comprehend the doctrine of dependent origination. The more faith we have in this teaching of the Buddha, the more our life can be settled — that is, based on wisdom with an adjustment in our mind and correction in our behavior. Sometimes we know our actions are heading towards the ultimate goal even though others may not understand us. This is fine. Our practice does not need the approval of others. Having understood the teachings and with the arising of wisdom within, we will find that there is nothing we need to escape or avoid. When we truly believe in causality, it is true liberation. Now you are not free because your confidence is less than one hundred percent. Sometimes people have a mindset of taking chances, thinking that even if they did many unwholesome deeds, there might be a some kind of force that can help them to avoid receiving the consequences. This mentality is not having belief in causality.

There are many unfortunate things that happen in daily life. If they happen to us, this certainly is the consequence of our actions and we must accept it. When we are able to accept it, we will be able to put it aside and let it go. If things have been smooth and nothing dramatic has happened to us, when death comes one day, the mental attitude with which we face death will be an indicator of how much we have practiced. It will be exhibited at the moment of death and nobody will be able to escape it.

When you see wandering thoughts in your mind during sitting, you cannot pretend they aren't there. You may fake something externally to conceal it, but in your mind, how is it possible to cheat on yourself? If you can observe wandering thoughts and establish the right view of causes and conditions, and be willing to accept this law, you can face yourself and have no desire to deceive yourself or others. Anything false will be recognized one day and truth will become obvious. So we must first establish right attitude. Being clear about the teachings will generate more faith. With faith, wisdom will arise and help us to adjust our mentality.

We know there are aspects that Buddhist and non-Buddhist (or "outer path") practices have in common. For example, both employ the technique of observing the breath. The practice of Chan can lead one to enter a state of samadhi. Other approaches of practice can do the same. In observation of the breath, there is subtle energy moving in the body. This can also happen to people who practice the art of qigong. However, Buddhist practice emphasizes cultivation of the mind. Therefore body adjustment is not the ultimate focus in Chan practice. The aim of our practice is not samadhi itself, unlike qigong with which practitioners may manipulate chi and demonstrate their special ability. Similarly, even though concentration in samadhi can be powerful, if awareness is lacking, one is unable to do contemplation. Thus Buddhist practice does not advocate entering deep samadhi. When meditative absorption reaches a certain degree, we turn to the practice of contemplation.

Often in contemplation we find our theoretical foundation is not solid enough or sufficently complete to be penetrative, and a person does not even know how to begin the contemplation. In order to perceive causes and effects and the phenomenon of dependent origination through the flow of life, one must first comprehend the doctrine of the law of causality. In other words, it is essential to establish a foundation of right view through study. With right understanding, one can then progress in contemplation. Without right knowledge, it is difficult to draw the right conclusion from observation.

Theoretical Foundation

Establishing right view requires long-term committed study of the Dharma, and it is not sufficient to just read Buddhist texts — one must comprehend the teachings through the reality of life. If one has only an intellectual understanding, it will not penetrate deep in the mind. In contemplation, only deep reflection will have the desired impact. In other words, when the mind is dwelling in a more subtle state, the teachings of Dharma should still be accessible in consciousness. Otherwise deeper contemplation will not have the necessary strength.

It is helpful to memorize some of the sutras and let them live in your mind. At the beginning you may not fully understand the text of the sutras as you try to memorize them. However, gradually the teachings will be ingrained in your consciousness and you will find the memorized sutra verses have their functions when you do contemplation. In memorizing the sutra, it is important to know the meaning of the text, and ponder, digest and reflect on them.

There are different approaches to deepening the understanding of Dharma. One is to establish a more complete system; another is simply to penetrate the core of the teaching. A complete system includes a wide range and variety of angles. Direct penetration to the core requires strength from the depth of practice. If you only know the core concepts, for example, of no-self, and have memorized some verses of the sutra without a thorough understanding of the meanings, you will not be penetrating the core. Some people need to take a wide and systematic approach and gradually enter the core of the teachings, while some others can take a more direct approach of deep investigation and entering the core of the teaching.

What most people lack in studying of the Dharma is not the methods for practice but rather the right view. As the Chan patriarchs often say, "the value is in seeing the truth, not in traveling" — at the critical stage, the direction and progress of practice is dependent on what view it is based on. Regardless of the stage of practice, if right understanding is complete and thorough, and as long as one can collect the mind and concentrate, the function of awareness can be turned to contemplation. In this way, one can practice following the right path step by step with certainty of success.

It seems that everyone has some knowledge when talking about right view. However, most people are unable to express or describe it clearly. Sometimes people read books in Buddhism, mostly for enjoying the gentle and sentimental aspects of the contents. When reading books that are more academic, it is as if their eyes are on the pages but their mind has gone elsewhere. If one is unable to read profound texts in Buddhism, it is difficult to establish right view.

Many people say, "They are only theories. Is it useful?" Yes. When you constantly think about it, it will be infused in your mind. Some of the theories may seem esoteric and subtle and require great focus in order to understand their meaning. And precisely because of this, you will not to want to skip over them. Books that are filled with romantic phrases or beautiful descriptions are very easy to glance through but in the end, how much of them touch you deeply and remain in your mind?

Some people reach a state of calm-abiding and want to do contemplation but do not know where to begin. This is due to the lack of right understanding of the doctrine, so they cannot penetrate and verify the Dharma and the practice. For example, from the arising and ceasing of wandering thoughts or breath, we observe the phenomenon of impermanence. But what is the deeper teaching that impermanence tries to tell us? The world is vast, what is the use of contemplating? Some people ask, "Impermanence is suffering — isn't contemplating on it more suffering?" or " Impermanence is suffering — what can we do?" If you have questions like these, contemplation will not go very deep — at the most it will stay at the arising and ceasing of the breath and the understanding that it is impermanent. When we do contemplation, what we are trying to see is the change or the true nature of phenomena, which is the intrinsic nature of all phenomena. Further, with this understanding one perceives no-self. This requires a thorough understanding about the doctrines of impermanence and no-self.

Sometimes we see an obvious, big or sudden change and we realize impermanence. However, what the Dharma teaches us is to observe the arising and ceasing in every instant or micro-instant. If we are not clear about the doctrine and do not truly comprehend it, our mind will not have strength in contemplation. In the third chapter "The Common Dharma of Five Vehicles" of the book The Way to Buddhahood, Venerable Master Yin Shun tells us that we need to have the right view from the very beginning of the path. Right view of what? Right view of the three aspects — good and evil, karma and retribution, past life and after life.

When we contemplate on good and evil, karma and retribution, and past life and after life, this is the understanding of the law of causes and effects. If we can deeply contemplate these principles, verify the truth in them, and apply them in our daily life, our confidence will become firm and we will not commit wrong deeds. If our understanding or mindset has a problem in practice, it will lead us in another direction, and as the idiom says, "a tiny difference will cause a parting of a thousand miles." Hence, it is very important to establish a solid foundation of right view.

Causality in Practice

All manifestation takes place according to causes and conditions. As far as practice is concerned, if the causes and conditions are not sufficient, it is impossible to obtain the sought-after result. Therefore accept your own level of practice and do not seek the result you desire; then you can be content. If you have two percent of energy, use two percent — better yet, use only one and a half and keep the other half as room for moving around a bit. Some people have only two cents but stretch to use five cents, with the other three borrowed from the bank. They then have to repay the interest. Without the ability to pay back, the debt will increase. So in practice, the concept of cause and effect is important. With right view, wisdom will manifest and you can adjust your life accordingly — otherwise one is overdrawn. For instance, if you feel lack of energy but you continue to force yourself, you will collapse. If we can understand the law of cause and effect, there is no need for many of our activities. Just practice sincerely, using whatever effort you can afford.

Actually the real impediment to practice is usually not that the method does not work, but rather our impatience. Without patience, no method can be successfully adopted because the wandering thoughts of impatience are coarser than the wandering thoughts of inability to use the method. Being unable to use the method is simply a fact, but if you add the affliction of impatience on top of that, it is creating karma, causing another cycle of confusion, karma and suffering.

Thus when you have difficulty using the method, face it and accept the fact. When you can accept the fact as it is, you stop generating new cycles of samsara. Your mind will slowly focus and the method will work. What is wrong with not sitting well? Do you fear that others might see it? Who has the leisure to watch you? Only you know whether you did well or not. Even if others did see it, so what? They cannot help you anyway!

In sitting we can see many things in our mind — all sorts of mindsets will come out. We need to see them clearly, face them with the law of causality, and eliminate unnecessary afflictions. Then we will be able to sincerely employ the method. When you can verify these principles, they will help you to adjust your understanding. This is wisdom. Without the understanding of cause and effect, your afflictions will continue to generate suffering and form bigger obstacles and you will be unable to apply the method well.

Sometimes things appear to us as if they are the consequences of another's actions. From the perspective of cycles of causes and retribution, however, what happens to us must have something to do with us. This being so, we ought to bear it, and face and accept the consequences. When our mind can be adjusted, the driving force of subsequent causes and effects will be lessened. For example, say there is a car accident and as a result, you end up with a broken leg. What are the causes and effects? It is a fact that the other driver hit your car. Even if they pay you hundreds of thousands dollars and have their driver's license revoked or even serve a few days in jail, can the breaking of a leg be undone? Of course we are not saying that we shouldn't handle this matter. From the standpoint of traffic laws and justice, we will deal with it, but at the same time we must face the fact of the broken leg.

Through accepting facts and being firm on the law of cause and effect, we can better adjust our attitude. If we investigate the root of anything, it is endless because the cycle of causes and effects is without beginning and without end. It is like a vast network going in all directions. When we can accept facts, unfortunate occurrences will make us grow in wisdom. If we cannot stop blaming others and ourselves, it is very painful. Not only does this not solve problems, but it also creates new problems.

What is the use of reading so many Dharma books? It is to constantly train our minds so that we have wisdom and the ability to transform vexations to bodhi no matter what happens. But in reality, often we lack confidence in the law of causality. We don't need our training to be one hundred percent perfect. Even fifty percent will be enough to make one live more happily. Take a look at our mind — when wandering thoughts are churning and a myriad of problems are manifesting, we know that we are still unable to eliminate them using the law of cause and effect, and that is why practice is more burdensome for us than others.

Truly, faking does not work in practice. One's depth of practice is reflected in one's behavior. If we have only three percent but want to show five, the two must be borrowed in order to make it up. In the end, when the truth is revealed, the three percent of practice is also gone. If we have three but use two, we have another one to use at any time. If we continue to practice sincerely, we may get from three to four. At such time, we still use only two or three percent, then we have enough resource in cultivation to face what happens in daily life. We can see in many refined practitioners that what they show is only part of their depth. Practitioners like this can sustain their practice and do not need to borrow from the bank.

Thus when you are having difficulty in applying the method or have leg pain, honestly face it. If it becomes unbearable, you may put down your leg for a bit. However, be considerate when you do so to avoid disturbing others. This is cultivation. If you cannot sit anymore, let the timekeeper know by raising your hand and go out for a walk. Even if you cannot keep it up and faint on your cushion, it is not so terrible. Do we need to care about our "face" in the Chan hall? It is unnecessary to force any result. Practice requires letting go. Whatever ability you have in practice, it is good enough. This is the mentality you need to examine in practice, for right attitude is very important and it directly affects your actions.

Avoid Going Astray

In addition to perceiving right view in contemplation, studying the Dharma consistently helps us to continue digesting and taking in. You really need to read more Dharma books and ground yourself in the practice because when you reach a certain stage, you will find that practice cannot deepen without theoretical foundation. Do not imagine that simply sitting on the cushion can naturally enlighten one. When you realize you are short in understanding or knowledge, try enhancing it.

On the other hand, some people find that they lack practice when their study has reached a certain place. They may feel unable to go into deep and subtle reflection since the condition of their mind is too coarse. In such cases, they can use the approach of calm-abiding to strengthen concentration. They can focus on where their reflection was stuck and try to penetrate it, and continue to keep going until understanding comes through.

Generally speaking, the lack of right view or inability to deepen the application of the method in practice is due to the lack of theoretical foundation. To continue practice without a good foundation makes it possible to go astray. Maybe you think that right view cannot help you take control of your afflictions or guide you to the right path, and that as long as you practice with diligence, it is okay. With such an attitude, even if your ability to practice has increased, it is no different from the outer path. Outer path practices can also cultivate samadhi. Some of these are even deeper than that of the Buddhist tradition for they only focus on concentration with the aim of attaining meditative absorption or gaining super-ability.

Some new religions now follow the outer path practices. Some of these are quite powerful; without these they are unable to attract and keep disciples following their teachings. They also have some spiritual sensitivity but without the Buddhadharma. To them, the Dharma is only intellectual knowledge, not useful as a guide for practice. Why do such sects have popularity and draw lots of followers but the Buddhadharma does not? It is because the Dharma teaches the followers about keeping precepts, generosity, and diligence in practice, and many people consider this troublesome. In the outer path practice, they do not have to keep the precepts; they can eat meat and drink alcohol. Their giving a bit of a magic touch to their teachings may have more immediately impact. Many people have such a mentality mainly because they do not believe in the law of causality. If they did, they would know that practice can only rely on one's own efforts. Even the disciples of the Buddha were no exception. They were not enlightened because they were disciples of the Buddha. Ananda served the Buddha for twenty-five years; only after the Buddha's parinirvana did he attain the fruits of an arhat.

Thus, the right view of the Dharma is extremely important. When we have complete understanding of the Dharma, as wandering thoughts arise in sitting, we will be able to see all of the principles of the teachings through these wandering thoughts. As the function of contemplation becomes stabilized, wandering thoughts will gradually subside and we can quickly grasp the core of the teaching. Based on that, our understanding about the Dharma will naturally become clearer because now it comes from subtler reflection and its penetration goes deep.

In practice we need to make ongoing adjustments. This helps us to move forward toward our aim of practice. Do not worry too much about this and that — just honestly face yourself, trust in the law of cause and effect, improve your weaknesses, and enhance your strength. Slowly you will make progress. You will have a better grasp of the method and know yourself better. Whether you cultivate samadhi or insight, being guided by the right view of Dharma will enable you to succeed step by step.

5

Suffering in Samsara

In practicing the meditation methods, when your ability to concentrate becomes stable so that your mind is not easily running with wandering thoughts, you can begin to observe them, investigate and reflect. Sometimes you may find that, when you concentrate on one object, wandering thoughts become weak and the ability to observe gets stronger. With this condition of mind you can begin the practice of contemplation.

Theory and Actuality

Generally speaking, direct contemplation following the doctrine of dependent origination is not easy to do because the mind that is concentrating on an object is not active in thinking. For instance, when one can follow the breath and the breath is subtle and deep, the mind likes to remain still without thoughts arising. This state of mind is stable. To drive it to be active again requires a bit of conscious effort. Therefore, having a deep understanding of the Dharma is essential because, in the end, contemplation is about investigating the nature of phenomena with the penetrating wisdom of the Buddhadharma.

Because the function of contemplation is based on the object of contemplation, when a thought that is the object of observation is empty, you will perceive that the function of observing is also empty. Furthermore, not only can you contemplate the phenomenon under investigation as empty, but you can also look at the function of observation itself. For example, in observing wandering thoughts — as the function of observing begins to operate, you find the objects being observed, which are thoughts, will diminish and then vanish. Slowly new thoughts will appear. At such times you find that behind the observing process there is another function of observing and there is layer after layer in the process. This is the phenomenon of alternating between the function of observing and what is being observed — a moment ago it was the function of observing, but going further, it is as if it itself is being observed by a deeper function which can itself go on deeper. In this process, we need to have a good grasp of the Buddhadharma. Otherwise you will have no clue as to where to go in this process of returning inwardly (or "Turning" as described in The Six Gates to the Sublime by Master Zhiyi.)

Even if you have not reached such a level, when contemplating that the object is empty and without a self, you should not stop at the meaning of the words — doing so will not help you realize the Dharma in contemplation. Take the investigation of arising and ceasing or impermanence as an example. If you only know that the word "impermanence" means change or that everything is a process of arising and ceasing without comprehending it, you will be unable to perceive it in your contemplation. Thus it is necessary to make an effort to study the Buddhadharma as well as to make an effort to verify the teachings in daily life.

All phenomena exist according to laws. What we know about the theory should not be separated from the experience of phenomena. Usually we see them as two separate matters because in our system of thinking we cannot connect them. Phenomena related to the sense faculties easily invoke emotional reactions which are in accord with the function of affliction. When we reflect on doctrines with logic, we understand that it is the phenomenon of dependent origination that takes place when causes and conditions are ripe. Typically our reactions are automatic because long-accumulated habits are our main stream of consciousness, and they easily appear as apparent emotions when we come into contact with external stimuli. Only after we notice that reactions have occurred do we use logical thinking to analyze them. Hence there seems to be a gap between the actual experience and the theory and we are unable to connect the two. This is why real comprehension of the doctrines involves experience. In other words, we need to know the reason behind what happens.

Usually reasoning itself is not so complicated. However, if we merely analyze the meaning of words, it becomes just a view or an opinion. Only with a period of deep investigation and reflection through practice can it become the main stream of our thinking or consciousness. This will then help us with seeing clearly the phenomenon of dependent origination — not only seeing the phenomenon but also understanding the principles beneath.

In studying Buddhism, it is not enough to merely know the words of noble truth that all phenomena bear the three seals of impermanence, no-self, and emptiness. This is why in his teachings, the Buddha put an emphasis on the arising and ceasing of phenomena. He taught that all manifested phenomena, our body and mind included, appear because of the ripening of causes and conditions — they arise, abide, change, and then perish. However, when we observe impermanence and no-self, we usually do not observe our own mind and body. Because of this, contemplating impermanence and no-self becomes a theory existing out there objectively instead of the truth on which our subjective function in daily life is based.

In observing our mind and body we can actually see the essential doctrine of the four noble truths in the Buddha's teachings — suffering, the cause of suffering, extinguishing suffering, and the way of extinguishing suffering. This foundational doctrine is very important. Without following this sequential aspect in studying, our understanding about impermanence and no-self is very limited. Why? If we do not perceive suffering from the reality of our life, we will not experience the phenomenon of cyclic existence in actuality and, as a result, we won't be able to investigate the root cause of suffering that drives the cyclic movement. If we cannot see clearly the causes and effects in the world of the mundane, it will be impossible to see the causes and effects of the supra-mundane — if you do not know your body and mind, what is being liberated? What do you cultivate? Where is your practice going? What is the goal? If you cannot see suffering in the cyclic existence of your life, you will not know why you want liberation. Therefore it is necessary to perceive the cyclic existence of an ordinary being like ourselves, for only then can we further practice towards the ultimate liberation of an enlightened being.

Usually we do not have sufficient knowledge about our mind and body. This is why we must clearly see our wandering thoughts in sitting meditation. Wandering thoughts contain the content of suffering and the cause of suffering. They are the actual conditions in our everyday life that create the suffering which is the process of karma and retribution. When karma and retribution are in operation, they include the afflictions in our mind. We do not feel them when there is no external cause and condition to ignite them. For example, someone has a craving for food — sometimes this is not evident because there is no favorite food in front of them to entice them. In many circumstances, we may feel we do not have anger or affliction but once being criticized, afflictions jump up immediately.

The phenomena reflected in our wandering thoughts include our daily life as well as the world we live in. The span of the world can be small or big — as small as the Chan hall where we all sit right now, or as big as our society, our country, the earth — it can extend to the galaxy. Although the impact of things far away seems indirect to us, sometimes it can be huge. Much of what happens in this world has an impact on us. Sometimes our actions affect not only our immediate surroundings but also the world. In other words, within the world in which we live, each individual existence is interrelated with others. When small incidents happen in our life, usually our choice of action is based on the situation we are in at that moment. However, what happens in the small environment is related to the bigger environment. For instance, our way of thinking and that of the people in the West are different since our inherited cultural traits are not the same. It is inevitable that our behavior is influenced by local factors. Similarly in smaller environments — someone in our family may not respond to what happens the same way as we do. Otherwise there would be no such thing as some families living in harmony while others live in chaos. The atmosphere created by the entire environment of functions of each individual in interaction varies and therefore cannot be neglected. At the same time, our actions also fuse back into our consciousness and make the cycle continue. Thus, understanding of doctrines must go hand in hand with the actuality of our experiences.

Pain and Suffering

Although the pain we sense in the body is apparent, the suffering that Buddhism talks about refers more to the pain in our mind. The source of this pain includes the impact of our immediate environment upon which we depend. If we cannot clearly see ourselves in real life, what are we talking about in practice? How do we practice? We say that we must root out the afflictions, but where are they? Why do we need to cleanse them? If we cannot investigate the operation and flow of our suffering, why do we practice? Only when we can perceive the actual flow of suffering and want liberation, do we undertake real practice.

Human life is made up of causes and conditions. Its existence is a process of cyclic movement. In the process, we see suffering and we say that life is suffering. Some people who have reached a certain level in studying Buddhism feel that they can go no further. This is because they cannot realize the truth through experience of daily life and actually practice it. It is no different than for those who always feel the world is grey and negative when they talk about suffering, or those who, as soon as they think of practice, immediately want to escape suffering through the method, imagining that they will no longer suffer if they sit in meditation.

Physical pain due to illness is just a sensation. The reason we suffer is because when we experience unpleasant stimulation and our consciousness is affected, anger or worry arises in our consciousness and we feel suffering. This type of suffering is on the surface — the kind of pain felt by the sense faculties. It is the only level we can sense. Why do we say the cycle of birth and death is suffering then? If we observe from a more subtle aspect, it is not merely the sensation of pain. In sitting meditation, those who practice well can observe their leg pain and investigate the subtlety of it so they do not necessarily feel suffering. We know that sense faculty, objects, and consciousness together generate the so-called contact. Only when there is a feeling does the sensation of pain become suffering. When suffering is felt, there is a resistance, and the emotion of anger or aversion arises that drives our reactions.

Hatred and love are two sides of the same coin. If one does not cling to their body, pain will not create suffering. As long as there is a feeling, there will be clinging. With clinging, there will be grasping. After grasping, there will be becoming and birth, aging and death. Suffering is not only the feeling after contact takes place, but also the problems following the arising of feelings. Suffering is the consequence or retribution. With suffering, there is confusion. Because of ignorance, we continue to create karma which causes more suffering. This is the cycle.

Therefore, real suffering is in the sea of samsara, the continual outflow of ignorance. When we get something we wanted, we feel happy, don't we? Can suffering be avoided when we feel happy? Are we forever happy after getting what we wanted? Can this happiness never leave us? Is there such a thing as an eternal unchanging happiness? No. However, if something sad or painful happened to us last year, we could still be thinking about it now — it can cause us to suffer for the rest of our life as though suffering follows us forever.

There is an analogy in the classic texts — when we have a wound and it is itchy, we apply some medicine, and we feel happy when the itch stops. Our happiness is like this — life is suffering in the cyclic existence. Sometimes when our craving is being satisfied to a degree, we feel happy. But how long can such happiness last? How long can the effect of medicine last? When the strength of medicine is gone, the wound will be itchy again. So in life, what we consider happiness is short lived and often cannot be sustained for a long time. Similarly, things that make us happy also lose their effect after they have been repeated a few times. When I was young, I played a lot of games. Sometimes I loved to play with a particular toy but after a couple of weeks, I lost interest. Then I went fishing, and later played with a kite. At the beginning of each activity it was exciting and I felt happy. Once the newness was gone, I lost interest and looked for something else to do. Our sense faculties are like this. Constant stimulation becomes dull, and it is not that pleasurable. Thus we often find that the fun we seek is short lived. This is because we have the mindset of gain and lose, and attachment to the self. After getting something, we want to own it. And not long after getting it, we want to throw it away. If we investigate our life deeply and learn about what happens in this process of cyclic existence, we will understand that this is samsara, and it will help us to stop the operation of affliction.

Causes of Suffering

The function of consciousness is accustomed to clinging to the past, present and future. When past, present and future are linked in our mind, samsara will continue, and it is suffering. For instance, you sit well in meditation today then suddenly you remember something that happened two months ago, and your mood is totally changed. Sometimes we experience things like this — when everyone is happily chatting and laughing, all of sudden someone says something that reminds you of something in the past. Your face immediately drops and the entire atmosphere is dimmed. That something happened a long time ago, but you are unable to put it down and you keep clinging to it. As long as samsara is in operation, such suffering will continue to have an impact on you.

Perhaps you will say, "If it is as simple as this, I will just think about happy things and then I will be happy." Strangely, unhappy things keep a tight hold of you and do not let you go while the happy memories are forgotten, and you feel unhappy again. Unhappy things have passed but in your mind you continue to recycle them and they get strengthened. When you recall things from the past, you add current emotions to it. If you continue like this, it is impossible for samsara to end because you keep driving the momentum. When suffering appears, all you want to do is escape or eliminate it immediately, but you constantly generate more karma that bears unwanted consequences.

Often people take such an approach when they face suffering. For instance, when leg pain in sitting is unbearable, you put down your legs that were in a crossed sitting position and focus on the breath. Actually if you can really concentrate on the breath, the leg pain will not bother you and will eventually disappear. But if you put down your legs and are still unable to employ the method and keep changing your sitting posture, the problem of leg pain is not solved and you are merely escaping. Most of the time people deal with suffering in this way.

Actually we can feel and sense that suffering is superficial in physical form because we actually feel it through the sense faculties. However, if it only stays as a contact, which is a function of the body that arises and ceases in an instant, and if we do not let it develop into a feeling, it will not cause suffering. Pain can cause the feeling of suffering because it is not only the function of the body faculty and body consciousness but has also become a perception and entered our consciousness. Perception will cling to past, present, and future and make the cycle endless. With such an endless cycle, leg pain becomes suffering when we hope it will not be painful again, or worry that it may become more painful. This is why even before sitting some people worry about leg pain. The legs are not sitting crossed and pain has not happened yet, so why worry?

Another common case is one in which a person sits well and expects the next sitting period to go well. About the past — we either regret it or miss it. About the future — we either worry or expect something. What about now? Now happens between past and future — what are you doing now? Are you thinking about the wonderful or not so wonderful things of the past, or worrying about bad things that might happen in the future? When will you be in the present?

We connect past and future and let it recycle. Everyday we are doing it. So when we sit down and meditate, all sorts of wandering thoughts arise and they are all clinging to the past and future. Although we see this tendency, we continue to drive from the past to the future. Sometimes we think a lot about the future. For some people, as soon as the retreat is over, the plan about next year has already been arranged. Our mind is in process like this. Thus the real suffering is a continual flow of ignorance, karma, and suffering.

In speaking about the great matter of birth and death and that samsara is suffering, we must understand it in context so that we know why we practice — it is to extinguish this suffering. Otherwise, in just reading the words about birth, aging, sickness, and death, some people do not feel this to be suffering. Is birth really suffering? We usually remember fun moments of our childhood; also some people feel happy when they are old; and there are people who are happy even with sickness — when being sick, they don't have to take care of anything — it is not bad. So sickness is suffering of the body but the mind may not be suffering. What about death? People usually are afraid of death. Perhaps it is really suffering. Otherwise why does it make people so fearful? Usually we only feel the suffering of birth, aging, and sickness on a sense level. Sensation is an important link in the cyclic flow of samsara, but it is not enough to just understand suffering from the aspect of sensation because it comes from contact which also has reasons behind it. Contact includes the functions of the six sense faculties, which are cognition and discrimination, as well as the external environment — the external six stations. These functions exist with the compound of body and mind of the individual, only then is there a contact. Contact causes sensation. After that it develops into craving, clinging, becoming, and the whole process as a cycle.

Therefore the suffering of parting with loved ones is not that the loved ones have departed. We also feel suffering when we cannot avoid those whom we dislike. It is not simply like this but it contains many cyclic processes before that. Why does one love this person? Why does one dislike that person? There are many reasons. We often fixate on our feelings, mostly feelings of suffering. This is why we look for things to fulfill various cravings. For example, we feel suffering when parting from loved ones, so we try not to part; we hate those whom we dislike, so we try to avoid meeting them. Doing so makes it seem that suffering is gone temporarily. But this is superficial liberation on the level of feeling as it has neglected the arising of feeling, which includes the process of cyclic movement. Continuing to flow out of ignorance, it will create more subsequent causes and conditions.

If you have sufficient theoretical foundation when contemplating wandering thoughts, you can see these phenomena clearly and verify the teachings of the Buddha. The Buddha left household life in order to understand the problem of birth, aging, sickness and death. In the beginning, he encountered many outer path teachings, which only temporarily answered his inquiries about suffering. For example, after entering a samadhi state, many painful feelings can be dropped. But upon emerging from meditation, the problems will return because this is a problem of cyclic process. If the roots are not cut out, the suffering will not cease. When the Buddha was finally enlightened under the bodhi tree, he perceived the phenomenon of samsara and because of that, ignorance — which is the essential driving force — was eradicated.

All suffering is caused by ignorance. To eliminate suffering, one must see that feelings are suffering. Why would feeling take place? Because of contact. Why does contact cause the feeling of suffering? Behind the operation of feeling is form, the six doors of the senses. Seeing this clearly, when contact takes place — if we have wisdom — we do not let feelings arise out of ignorance or cling to them, and thus ignorance is extinguished and all that follows will be extinguished. What the Buddha saw at enlightenment is this whole cyclic process of dependent origination. This process can go across the three periods of time — past, present and future. Actually through everything that happens, we can see the process of dependent origination.

To observe wandering thoughts is to see dependent origination in each incident of arising and ceasing. If you can see it clearly, you will know that the main driving force of samsara is ignorance and clinging. Seeing this in daily life, it is the same. The gain and loss in daily life is all the flow of samsara, starting from contact.

Through practice, wisdom can manifest. If our actual experience and theory mutually verify each other, when contact takes place, not only will we see the causes of phenomena but we will also clearly see the characteristics of the Dharma of dependent origination. Then we will not drive the force further, since from dependent origination we see emptiness and no-self. Having eliminated the view of self and attachment to the self, we will not push forward the force of samsara. This is the extinguishing of samsara. To perceive such dynamics of samsara, we must observe our body and mind in daily life. In our Buddhist study about the six doors, form and perception, form is the individual existence of compounded body and mind; perception is the function of discrimination, and the six doors are the doors to the external world. The six stations are the various external conditions. All these are combined in generating a contact. At the instant of contact, does ignorance arise or is it extinguished? This is how you must observe samsara; if not, samsara will continue.

Often when suffering takes place we relate it to ignorance and continue its flow and thus become confused. With confusion we create karma and more suffering. Because what we can observe is the result of suffering — we are unable to experience the entire relationship of cause and effect or see it clearly. To have wisdom, not only do we need to see cause and effect, but also to see that the nature of dependent origination is empty. After understanding the law of cause and effect, some afflictions will be eliminated because of wisdom. However, such wisdom still lacks strength. Not until the driving force is cut off at each moment of contact will wisdom be full of power.

Eliminating Suffering

Even though in daily life we create karma, the cyclic process can be slowed down with the observing of cause and effect and by understanding the doctrine of dependent origination. At such times we can use the Dharma and the wisdom derived from observing our body and mind to investigate what happens and to see clearly the phenomenon of suffering and retribution. For example, when observing wandering thoughts, many memories of the past appear. If you use the principle of impermanence and no-self to analyze, you can put them down without recycling them. This lessens the strength of samsara. This is not cutting off at the root because you have not actually realized no-self nor has the cyclic force fully stopped, so they may appear again. But the impact it has on you is no longer as strong. If you practice well, and your mind can concentrate inwardly using impermanence and no-self to further penetrate and resolve the issue, the dynamics of samsara will be lessened even more. The Buddha did so in his practice and eventually eliminated suffering.

In the beginning it may take a long time for us to do this, but gradually it takes less time because wisdom grows more sharp and more powerful. Once contact takes place, wisdom quickly arises and becomes the main stream of thoughts in our daily life. Thus if we can keep fusing the Dharma in our mind and make it the viewpoint in our dealing with everyday affairs, our mentality can be adjusted to the right path. When things happen, this central function of mind will arise first.

We must constantly be mindful. If ignorance has not been completely eliminated and wandering thoughts are still hidden in subtle areas, when they arise, many things can be adjusted before samsara begins cycling. Even though the consequences of what happened in the past cannot be avoided, with wisdom the chances of their recurring can be reduced. Practice extends this power to daily life, using wisdom to handle things and to reduce suffering in the future. Now we do not have the strength to handle it because we carry past karma to the present and current karma to the future. When a series of impacts roll over us, our mind is flooded. Usually our mind is flooded by lots of wandering thoughts and continues to create new momentum. So first we must raise awareness in our mind and not be dragged away by wandering thoughts. It is like pulling yourself out of a wave so that you can observe it clearly. Use the method of calm-abiding in meditation to depart from wandering thoughts and strengthen your mind. When your mind has strength, then you can observe wandering thoughts and see their functions clearly. With clarity, you can start to use wisdom in handling daily life and eventually eliminate ignorance.

Having directly verified and realized the true cause of suffering, you will know the importance of practice in ending it. If you fixate only on the phenomena of feelings or the coming-and-going, the problem is unresolved and will always be there. It is like moving the leg or injecting anesthesia or cutting off the leg when there is leg pain — it is an ascetic way of the outer path, which only tries to extinguish suffering but not to find the cause of suffering. What is the cause of suffering in this case? Very simple — it is the lack of practice! Often we use a complex approach to handle things, so it is still in the domain of suffering. If we know where the problem lies and start treatment from the root cause, the problems may not become so serious.

Where does the feeling of suffering come from? It does not happen only when feeling occurs, because each feeling contains many causes and conditions within it. We must see the cause in order to know how to approach it, and know why the Buddha said cyclic existence is suffering and the process of impermanence and change is suffering. After knowing this we can further eliminate it. Once we know that practice is to eliminate suffering, right view can be established and guide us towards liberation. To truly understand the process of suffering requires ongoing study, and that we verify and realize the truth through actual experience.

Sometimes even though they know the methods for practicing contemplation, some people still do not know how to begin. This is due to a lack of right view. Others know the doctrine of impermanence and no-self but cannot employ the practice method. This is because the understanding of

Dharma is not firm or deep enough. If you know this area is weak in your practice, adjust and strengthen it accordingly. Of course, this takes time. Practice takes time. Establishing right view takes time. Thus, do not expect that after a seven-day retreat all problems will be solved and everybody will return home enlightened. It requires ongoing practice in and out of retreat, time after time, in order to accumulate the provisions for deepened practice.

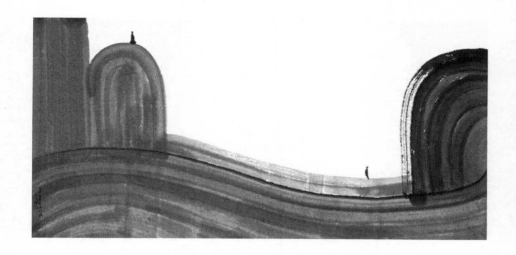

6

Between Goal and Actual

If one enters Chan practice through the gateway of study, at some point one might feel their actual practice is lacking. To enter the cultivation of wisdom, one must go through the gateway of "calm-abiding and contemplation" or "silent illumination". If through study, the establishment of right view is relatively thorough and practice is stabilized, one can practice contemplation based on the doctrines. Without these, contemplation will remain pretty much on the surface and one will not be able to penetrate to any depth. Some practitioners have some knowledge about the Dharma or deep understanding about their own personality, or they do well in sitting meditation, and they sometimes experience unexpected mental states or illusions. If these states appear, without the Buddhadharma as guidance, they may be uncertain as to whether these are in accord with the Dharma. At such critical moments, complete understanding of the Dharma is extremely important. Only through a practice based on the contemplation of right views can wisdom manifest..

Wisdom Is Not In Words

Even if one reads Dharma books, is familiar with Buddhist concepts, has memorized verses, or has verified the teachings through other systems of knowledge – without actually practicing and applying pracite to daily life one cannot penetrate deeply. Detailed investigation through practice into the operation of our body and mind is essential for comprehension of the doctrine of impermanence and no-self. When we are able to see that the form of life is the composition of the five elements (earth, water, fire, wood, metal), we will be able to understand the doctrine of dependent origination.

Life itself provides us with a constant source of conditioned arising and ceasing phenomena which have no permanent form or substance. Because each incident of cause and condition changes constantly, the phenomena that consist of incidents also arise and cease continuously. From observing such a process we find that, within phenomena, there are other causes and conditions that form a complex network. With such observations we can understand impermanence and no-self through the real construction of life, and can verify the doctrine of dependent origination. Then from there, the core of the Dharma – the noble truths, or the three seals of impermanence, no-self, and emptiness or nirvana – can be established. Only then do we truly know what impermanence and no-self are.

Most commonly, we merely understand the words of the doctrine. For example, the Heart Sutra mentions "emptiness" in different places. In the beginning it says, "The five skandhas are empty" (the five elements are empty). Then it tells us, "All dharma is empty of forms; it does not arise nor does it cease; not tainted nor pure; not increasing nor decreasing." Then, it says, "Emptiness is without eye, ear, nose, tongue, body, and mind." Reading these over and over, we do not know what this "emptiness" is really talking about. Although we can memorize and recite this sutra fluently, over and over we are merely circling around the words without knowing their meaning. It says, "Form is not different than emptiness; emptiness is not other than form; form is emptiness; emptiness is form." Then it says, "Feelings, volitions, perceptions are the same way." What does it really mean? Why is it followed by "All dharma is empty in form?" What we see with our eyes is apparently arising and ceasing instantly. Why does the sutra tell us "no arising, no ceasing?" What does this mean? Why does it say "emptiness does not arise nor cease" but we see the manifested phenomena arise and cease? Can we clearly and thoroughly understand these from the phenomena of our daily life – from our body and mind?

Next the Heart Sutra says "no eye, ear, nose, tongue, body, mind; no form, sound, smell, taste, touch, and thought." This is talking about the six sense faculties and the six stations. What do the six sense faculties mean? What do the six stations mean? How are they related to us? The sutra then tells us, "no realm of eye...and perception." What does it mean? How are they relevant to us? Why do scriptures use negation when talking about emptiness? These sense faculties or physical organs are what we obviously use in daily life. Why are they being negated as non-existent?

Actually, the five skandhas, the twelve stations, the eighteen realms are talking about how the world in which our body and mind reside is composed. How do these phenomena operate in cyclic existence? It is according to the law of dependent origination. From this law of conditioned arising and ceasing, we penetrate to the truth of impermanence and no-self. No-self appears as impermanence. Summarizing them we use the word "emptiness" to express it. This requires deep understanding. If we have clear comprehension of the doctrine, we will clearly understand the core of dependent origination, which is the nature of all dharma — it is empty and without a self. Then we can employ it in contemplation.

If we only understand the words, contemplation will be shallow at the level of words only. Of course it is still useful at this level because it has the effect of purifying our mind with the Dharma. Although not deeply penetrating, it is fine since studying itself is a process going from shallow to deep. However, we should not remain at the level of superficial understanding, and we should know the importance of self-awakening.

Accepting Facts

If we firmly believe in the law of cause and effect, in contemplation we can apply it to observing phenomena and our life. Often our sitting reflects our state of mind, and this reflects our understanding. If we do not practice regularly but rather create lots of karma out of ignorance, our meditation will manifest as wandering thoughts. When wandering thoughts arise, the method we use in practice is difficult to apply. This is cause and effect. When you find that in your mind there are more unwholesome thoughts than wholesome thoughts, this is also due to cause and effect. And in this case, obstacles will be more prominent in practice. Why? Because the appearance of unwholesome thoughts will create distractions. Even being distracted by wholesome thoughts is an impediment. Therefore, you should try to bring your attention back to the method.

We often say that we believe in cause and effect but many times we do not want to accept the fact that we do not practice well with the method. With such a mentality, various behaviors show up in the Chan hall. Accepting this as fact is an indication of accepting causes and effects and acknowledging that there is a problem that causes obstacles in our practice. By doing this, we can make adjustments accordingly. Some people do not want to accept fact, thinking that their practice should not be that bad. Actually, how good one's practice is, is not determined by oneself but by the law of cause and effect. Nobody wishes themselves to have a sloppy practice. When coming to a retreat, we all hope to overcome obstacles and realize enlightenment by the time we go home. Who does not want this? However, just because we have established such a goal does not mean that we can reach it immediately.

In daily life, it is the same. When unpleasant or undesirable things happen to us and we do not want to accept these, we suffer more since resistance causes more afflictions. If we do not solve it, it creates a new cycle of suffering. Thus, the extent to which we believe in cause and effect will be revealed. The appearance of result is due to the fact that causes and conditions are ripe – the result is originated from the cause. We hear stories about students committing suicide by jumping from high buildings because they did not do well in school exams. They do this because they do not want to accept the fact that they failed the exams. Actually, the exam is not only an individual karmic result – it also has "common karma", which includes situations such as the fact that the testing questions in the exam are not those that the student had prepared for. In such a case, what can you do? It is a fact, and not accepting it cannot change the fact. But most people do not want to accept facts. Even practitioners in Chan retreats behave like this – they do not want to accept their own current condition of practice. We often tend to think of ourselves as better than what we are. This is normal. However, when cause and effect manifest, we are shown the actual conditions. If we do not accept this fact, we suffer.

The most common cause of our creating suffering is anxiety. Why are we anxious when we cannot apply our method in sitting meditation? It is often actually not as bad as we imagine, but we do not want to accept the fact that we did not do as well as we had hoped. When we face it with an attitude of unacceptance, practice becomes worse because impatience is a coarse wandering thought that interferes with practice. Hence, how we face problems depends on our attitude towards the law of cause and effect. If you believe in it, you will be willing to accept the fact and make adjustments accordingly. For example, you can be better prepared by practicing regularly at home before going to a retreat. When you cannot do well with your method, being able to accept the fact with ease will reduce the pressure and anxiety in your mind.

Another common issue is that, when practice is not going well and one is unwilling to accept that fact, one keeps creating a fantasy in their head. For example, when one did not sit well, one dreams of sitting well. If one sits fairly well, one guesses what state they have reached or at which stage of dhyana they are. This is covering up the fact. Sometimes, if one is lacking self-awareness, the problem of "escalated arrogance" shows up. When one sits and bodily energy of chi starts to move, one might think perhaps it is the eight sensations (restlessness, itching, buoyancy, heaviness, coldness, heat, roughness, smoothness) that the ancient texts talked about.

As you may know, when practicing breath counting and entering samadhi of the form realm, adjustment in the body does take place. At such time, the inner body may experience the eight sensations mentioned above. We can treat chi movement as one of the sensations but this is very coarse since it is in the transition stage before first dhyana. This kind of sensation is for helping us adjust the body and it enables us to settle on the method. When the body is in a coarse condition, practice does not go well, so chi moves in order to adjust to it. During this adjustment, many unknown or hidden physical issues may come to the surface. After the adjustments, one can feel that the bodily condition becomes better.

In the samadhi state prior to the first dhyana, there is complete stillness. At this time, movement in the body is very subtle — one feels light, at ease and comfortable. If one feels a sort of force moving, it is not in samadhi because, in entering that state, the body in the realm of form has been well adjusted. While progressing towards samadhi in the realm of form, the mind is in a subtle state; however, the body is still coarse. It takes some adjustment to help settle the body with this subtle state of mind since the mind cannot be without form, and form and mind must be in harmony. The body adjusts itself until they are in harmony. So when entering samadhi of the form realm, the principal or directional karma from the past cannot change or be altered, but one's inner subtle state can be adjusted.

After this stage, those who practice qigong will talk about "channeling of the meridians". But in the classic text of Master Zhiyi, "An Explanation of the Dharma Gateway of Dhyana Paramita", the discussion on the eight sensations is not entirely from the angle of meridians. It is a type of chi, but it is subtle. If one still feels something is blocked in the body and needs to push through, this is coarse, which is adjusting the body in the desire realm. Under such conditions, do not delude yourself by thinking you have entered some sort of state. In the state of samadhi, the body is well adjusted and the sensation that appears is very subtle. One can feel subtle movement inside of the body like a very gentle electric current which permeates the entire body. If this current is only in a part of the body, such as the feet or head, etc. it is something else. Will a practitioner experience all of the eight sensations? Not necessarily. Some people only experience one or two while other sensations are not obvious to them.

We need to have a certain degree of understanding about our body. However, there is no need to guess what kind of state exists when one has body movement. Just focus on the method, and the mind will be more and more subtly adjusted. Guessing is coarse and meditation can regress to a condition that existed prior to entering samadhi because the observation is too strong. Thus, if you find yourself involved in a guessing game, simply refuse to play it.

When practice has reached the state of stillness, the mind cannot be too coarse. Hence do not use force to push it. When you begin the method of counting the breath, you may make an effort to pull back your scattered mind. When practicing "following the breath", with even the slightest push, your mind can fall back to the coarse condition. If there is still awareness knowing the mind is moving like this, do not guess what state it might be in. If you do this, it is very easy to fall into the hindrance of "escalated arrogance". In guessing, you might be hindering yourself by thinking "This part is channeled, or that part is channeled." If you go back and forth like this, by the time you emerge or exit from meditation, nothing is being channeled — it is only your imagination!

It has been mentioned earlier that, when chi moves, it can sometimes become a habit — you give it the hint to move and it will move. Which is saying, as long as you know the technique of chi movement, such as chi-gong practice, you can manipulate chi movement. It is the same with sitting meditation — if the mind thinks the body will move, the body can actually move. Thus we must have self-awareness, which is to keep in line with the law of cause and effect. When you understand the conditions of your body and mind, in seated meditation you can see the reaction of the body and mind, especially when thoughts float through. Escalated arrogance will hinder your practice.

Accepting the fact of whatever your condition is, adjust your mentality with patience. It is fine that the method does not work well for a time. If a leg hurts, with the mind of acceptance, it will not be that difficult to bear. Some people do not feel bad or impatient when there is leg pain; instead, they feel happy. Anxiety comes with the feeling of failing to use the method. By not accepting, one becomes more disturbed. Often we cannot control our mind. This reflects a lack of self-mastery. So even though people know they should not be anxious, when they sit and the method does not immediately work, they begin to feel impatient. The more such situations occur, the worse it becomes.

It is better to accept the fact. If you are totally unable to use the method, go let the timekeeper know and take a walk outside or get up and do prostrations. Do not be ashamed or feel that you are "losing face". When you cannot use the method, what use is it to try to save face? It is better to take a walk and prostrate, relax a bit, and not try to force it. Some conditions are adjustable, which require you to face them. If you are unwilling to face these, others cannot help you. So trust the causes and conditions no matter where you are in terms of wisdom, the more you trust these, the more wisdom will arise.

Accepting Others

Whatever happens has its causes and conditions. In interacting with others, if we feel mistreated, we may believe that the other person is not nice to us. However, was it us who first mistreated them or the other way around? It is hard to say. Even if they did mistreat us, there must be some pre-existing reasons. Causes and effects are not necessarily two-dimensional. From the time perspective, there are "before" and "after" and from the spacial perspective, there are common existing causes and effects. If we can accept such facts, it means that it is not merely the problem of others — we ourselves have responsibilities. When we are willing to take responsibility, the mentality is shifted, and we can understand that the mistreatment is our own imagination. If we do not feel what happened is mistreatment, it is solved, and the knot in the mind is gone. For example, you have been thinking you are right and the other person was wrong, but you forgive the other person. This is the wisdom of accepting others. If you reflect and realize you had made the first mistake, would you still blame the other person? So adjustment is like this, and this kind of mentality is adjustable. If such a knot is not resolved and stays in your mind, it becomes more and more solid and real, and it hinders practice.

Why do some behaviors become habits? Why are our clinging and attachment to the self so tight and deep? It is due to such knots being accumulated. Why is there the suffering of meeting with those whom we dislike? It is also due to accumulation. Every time we see the other person, the feeling of dislike increases a bit. Seeing that person another time, adds one more layer of hatred. After a long time, the hatred is solidified. The more solid it is, the more difficult it is to untangle. If we notice such problems at the time of affliction and do not fixate on them, things are actually not as serious as we imagine. Often we neglect the fact that in interaction with others, the standpoint of each person is different — we think it is this way, others may not think so, and often there are conflicts.

Thus in facing problems, we should look at them through the law of cause and effect. In addition to time perspectives, there are also spacial causes and effects. With understanding of such interrelatedness, we can broaden our views and see beyond any limited timeframe. If this adjustment is done well, having deep understanding about it, especially from the perspective of impermanence and no-self, many things can be put down and let go. Although we do not have enough wisdom to immediately solve problems, they can be transformed. On the contrary, if we let affliction continue to develop, on one hand it becomes more solid. On the other hand, its recycling force becomes stronger and stronger. If we try to solve it in a timely fashion, lessening the force of recycling, it will not become solidified. This is helpful in solving inner conflicts.

Practice is to help us see these issues. The more we understand and correctly grasp the principle of cause and effect, the more relaxed and open minded we will be when looking at things. Some people may think, "This is obviously letting ourselves be taken advantage of!" In practice, we must have a longer range view. We do not hold expectations about the future and we believe in cause and effect. The other person may not wish to resolve the conflict, but we can start with ourself! When we begin to transform, it is already resolving it. With sufficient strength of positive attitude, if the interrelationship still exists, our response may affect the other person. We must begin with ourself. It is possible that before we have been able to adjust ourself that the other person has already adjusted and forgives him or herself. So if we are truly making adjustments in our mind, slowly some stubborn habits can be dissolved, positive attitude and mentality enforced, and we can feel strength in our mind. With such practice of mindfulness, we will find that the capacity of our whole body and mind is changed. This is the progress in mind cultivation.

As wisdom keeps arising, we can see problems more clearly. If we can do further introspection, eventually we can find that there is really no self. If we can, from this perspective, examine what happened in the past, it is easier to let go of suffering because from the perspective of impermanence, what made us angry has passed. Since it has passed, if we continue to be angry, it is because we have carried it with us. We connect past and present and carry them with us all the time, and we suffer.

There is a story in the school of Chan. Two monks, a master and disciple, were traveling together. At one point the master carried a woman across a river. The disciple could not sleep for a few nights and finally asked the master, "As a monk, we are not supposed to touch the body of women. How could you carry a woman across the river?" The master answered, "I have put her down after crossing the river, but you are still carrying her (in your mind)!" Similarly, people seem to have so many burdens. Isn't that because we carry them? When you cannot use the method well in meditation, it is because of carrying too many things in your mind. These things come out as soon as you take the seat. No wonder these become hindrances! We must learn to slowly put them down, and this requires the practice of cultivating our mind.

In cultivating the mind, it is not only about facing problems but also solving them with wisdom. This is the process in contemplation as we clearly understand and believe in the law of conditioned arising and ceasing of cause and effect, and we accept the facts. The more we believe in cause and effect, the more we find the mind is widely open because wisdom has arisen. Believing in cause and effect a little, there is a little wisdom; believing in it totally, this is liberation.

Do Not Leave Practice at the Chan Hall

Now we can ask ourselves, how much do we believe in cause and effect? To believe in cause and effect requires interrelated verification of theory and experience. In seated meditation, when the mind carries lots of burdens, why not try applying the principle of cause and effect, which is no-self, to investigate it? In such a process, on one hand it has the effect of purification. On the other hand, we put the problem on the table and, through adjustment, free unnecessary burdens from our mind. If we can put down the past, we will feel light and at ease. Sometimes our mind is too heavy because we do not want to let go of the burden, or even find ourself saying something like "I have my reason for not letting go." What are the reasons? When you thoroughly investigate it, it is certainly due to a lack of trust in cause and effect. If your confidence in cause and effect is sufficient, wisdom will be there to help dissolve these burdens in your mind.

Practice can help in seeing this reality. Sometimes, when you sit, you feel a kind of lightness and ease and you think that your sitting is pretty good. But remember, if this only occurs in sitting, it means that it only has such an effect in meditation. You need to let this state continue after exiting from meditation so that it functions at all times — this is real cultivation. Feeling light and at ease in meditation is natural because the mind is quiet and relatively still. If when getting up from meditation, you feel anxious and uneasy or your mind feels heavy, this indicates that you have an ability to abide and concentrate in meditation but that wisdom is lacking. Only wisdom can help us keep the state of lightnness and ease in sitting as well as afterwards. Wisdom alone helps us to transform and lessen our mind's burdens. So if you go home after a retreat and wisdom did not truly increase, you will know it after a bit of time.

Some people can do well in the Chan hall, but after leaving the Chan hall, they carry all the burdens they brought to retreat back home again. It seems that for many people, when they are in retreat all their afflictions leave, but once they return home all of their problems reappear. They do not know where the practice in retreat has gone. They felt pretty good in practice but after leaving the Chan hall, they did not take the practice home with them. Wisdom grows gradually with practice. If one can carry the practice home, using wisdom to observe life situations, one can see things more clearly, and the approach one uses to handle situations will be more in harmony with the law of cause and effect. If affliction is the mainstream of one's thoughts in dealing with situations, one's dealings will operate with affliction. This is accumulated over a long time, and habits and affliction have been there all the time. When quieting down, the afflictions often have a very strong function. If we can constantly raise mindfulness, thoughts and mind can be in accord with the Dharma and the law of cause and effect, and slowly wisdom will become mainstream in our mind.

If we are ignorant and confused as "contact" with external objects takes place, it causes habitual reactions to recycle. If instead we have wisdom and ignorance ceases, the subsequent conditions will cease. As of yet, our wisdom has not reached such a level that we are able to use illuminating wisdom to shed light on it right at the instant of "contact." This requires actual realization in experience. Only then will we be able to do so. Now we are still in the stage of practice. We may have some experiences but not true realization. The deeper our experiences are, the closer wisdom will be able to function at the instant of "contact". In daily life, if affliction arises and we realize we have made wrong choices only when we quiet down after it has happened, it means that the function of wisdom has a time lag from the moment of "contact." Often the practice of repentance in Buddhism helps us resolve these issues.

For repentance to be sincere, it must be accompanied by the understanding of the principles of cause and effect, which means we accept our affliction and the knowledge that we can make mistakes. However when we do repent, usually it is only by reading the scripture or reciting "repenting our karmic actions" in Samantabhadra's Ten Great Vows. This does not deeply penetrate the mind. There is an ancient practice that provides a practical approach to repentenance and includes writing down what good or bad actions one did each day on a list of "Merits/Error". Some practitioners use the black and white pieces of Chinese board game — putting in a white piece when they did a good thing, putting in a black one when having a bad thought. In the evening they check and count the number of pieces, "Wow, there are fifty black ones but only five white ones!" This would remind them to make adjustments and improve their behavior. This is a form or practice which has its use. However, if we want wisdom to truly manifest, we need more of an internal practice. And this is the cultivation of the mind.

To raise the function of contemplation requires sufficient study and enough right view. Some people think that it is not necessary to practice at home, imagining that, as soon as they sit with legs crossed after entering Chan hall, their "sitting ability" will come! Do not dare to think that if one reads a lot of Buddhist books, learns some theory, and does some good deeds, one has a practice — It is not so.

Each person's condition is different, of course. Wherever you are at, adopt a suitable approach for yourself. If one has self-awareness, one can live more freely. We feel unhappy and bound because we know there is a more refined state of mind to look for but don't know how to reach it yet. In other words, we have expectations, and this type of expectation is good. It is the desire that a diligent practice needs — right thinking. Because there is a goal, we are motivated and will make effort to go towards it. But looking at our current condition, we see there is a distance to the goal, so we need to practice. If we cannot recognize suffering in our daily life, it is not likely that the goal of liberation can be established.

Those who study Buddhism have a type of suffering that is uniquely their own — it is that we know good and evil and we know to take the precepts as guidance, but we feel unable to follow them. There is a distance between what we know and what we are able to do. However, this is a motivating force that arises in our mind due to shame. Knowing the goal and our own shortcomings generates a driving force. In such a process we experience suffering because we feel we are not doing well enough.

It is the same with practice. We know there is a goal which we are not yet able to reach and consequently, there is the desire to continue pushing and improving. In the process, we must accept our own causes and conditions. Of course we want to go towards the goal, but in practice, one must return to the present condition. Present condition includes all facets of ourselves: our nation, cultural background, education, and our opinions as we grow up, etc. Whether they are good or not, they are a part of our conditions. Practice begins with self-awakening. Why do some people experience suffering when they cannot use the method? Often they have such an attitude because they have not accepted causes and conditions such as their shortcomings. If they can change this mentality, even though they do not clearly see the self, this self-awareness of the facts of causes and conditions will help them to see where their shortcomings lie and what needs improvement.

Some people experience lots of suffering in practice. A lot of the time this comes from family. For example, a person wants to practice but is afraid of their family's disapproval so they do not want to be seen in practice. What are they to do to practice? With the blessing of the family, practice can go more smoothly. Part of our personality comes from the family. So, to walk far on the Buddhist path, one must pay attention to one's relationship with family. If we can begin purifying ourselves, even if our family does not approve of it, they may be willing to withhold their judgement and make it easier for us to succeed with fewer obstacles. Where relationships exist there will always be causes and conditions because relationships do exist. In practice, causes and conditions have an important guiding function – the more firmly we believe in cause and effect, the more wisdom will grow.

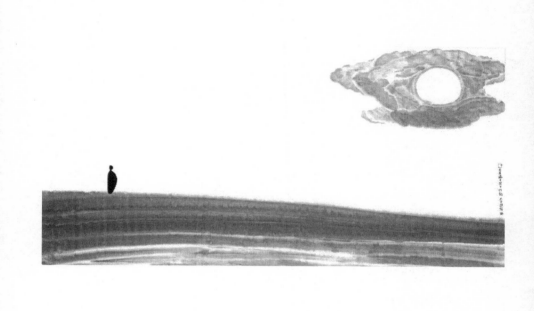

7

Self and No-Self

From the Buddhist perspective, Dharma is mainly about human beings. We can see this in the explanations of the doctrines, for example, those concerning the five elements, the twelve links of conditioned arising, or the eighteen realms, from the structure of body and mind of sentient beings. Although there is mention of other sentient beings, invariably the Dharma returns to the subject of human beings. In Chan practice, it is the human being as a whole person who is doing the practice.

Know the Self

Why do we practice? Because we want to solve the problems of our very own life. The composition of any individual includes the structure of body and mind, the environment in which the body and mind dwell, and the causes and conditions in interaction. The cultural background and education of a person can affect how they think and handle things. If we ignore these various causes and conditions, we cannot really see the problem of this individual whom we refer to as the "self".

Because the causes and conditions of each individual are not the same, a practice method employed by different people can have different results. Some people can skillfully apply it while others may have difficulty doing so. This is due to the fact that, in some cases, preparation was not done well and hence in meditation one does not have enough strength to collect the mind. For instance, someone is busy all the time — so busy that they do not find time for sitting or reading Dharma related books. Consequently, when they enter the Chan hall, various forms of obstacles appear. Also, in daily life, some people create bad karma through unwholesome actions which then affects them in meditation as some sort of obstruction.

If we think practice is complicated, it is because our individual form of life is composed of many complex causes and conditions. In practice, we try to see these causes and conditions clearly and learn to follow their natural course with acceptance. However, most often we simply don't want to accept facts but only wish to escape. The reason for wanting to escape, on one hand, is our unwillingness to accept karmic consequences, and on the other hand, it is our unwillingness to accept the self.

Eventually Chan practice is to break through the erroneous view of self and the attachment to it. But do we know what the self is? Where is this "I"? If we cannot even see this self clearly, how can we break the falsity of it? We need to first see and understand that the self, with an appearance of form, is nothing but a bundle of various causes and conditions. Then we verify the theory that this is true. If we claim "there is no self," but only know from theory that this self is the composition of various causes and conditions, then when we do contemplation in practice, the teachings will not have any strength to penetrate the mind. They will remain only words. This is what happens when one is unwilling to admit the problem and accept the consequences as one faces problems in daily life.

Our actions and thoughts all have causes and conditions. For example, people in Thailand think that if their child becomes a monastic, it is a good thing. Tibetan people hope their boys become lamas. Chinese people usually do not think in this way, and some parents would try everything to prevent their child from becoming a monk, which has something to do with the deep Confucian thinking in Chinese culture. On the other hand, some Westerners become monastics in the orient countries, but when they return to their homeland, without a monastery to practice in, they have to resume the work of a layperson because they cannot survive if they don't. If this is the condition in their society, they must follow its culture. Can you say that, after returning to lay life, they have lost the inspiration to practice? Who knows — maybe they can do better in sharing the Dharma as a layperson just as Jack Kornfield did. He is the author of "A Path with Heart: A Guide through the Perils and Promises of Spiritual Life" and was ordained in Thailand. When he returned to the United States, he disrobed, married, and had children. Additionally he obtained a Ph.D. degree in Psychology, and combining this with teaching meditation, he continues his Dharma work. In the Western society, he had to use such an approach to spread the Dharma. That is his particular "I" — a whole person, facing and accepting the fact of returning to the West and playing his role in the Dharma work in this way.

We should also understand our self in such a way in order to find the causes and conditions of our self. The thoughts we have are not something that suddenly appear out of nowhere — they are in conjunction with many causes and conditions. Over time, they form an imaginary self that is false. Why is it false? Because it is the combination of all the constantly changing causes and conditions. If we do not see these functions from the true nature of things, it is not easy for us to recognize this false self. This is why we often cling to the self.

Generally speaking, every person is an aggregation of causes and conditions — this is the false self. However, everyone's causes and conditions are different. We need to know our own causes and conditions so we can see where our problems in practice lie and what we can do to eliminate or overcome the difficulties. For example, in seated meditation, due to physical conditions, one person can use a method that we cannot use because we do not have such conditions, so we can only recognize it as an observation. If someone has strong passion in the body, he may use the method of observing impurity of the body. If you have strong anger or hatred and you use the same approach, the anger may become stronger and you will be unable to adopt this method properly. You should, instead, employ the practice of loving-kindness to counteract the habit of anger.

When one's mind is soft, a method can usually work well. If one's mind is stubborn, the Dharma cannot easily penetrate. For instance, some people can use the method of counting the breath for only a few days and they get it.

This is because their mind is not too complex to adopt the method. But why can't you do it? Maybe because your mind is too scattered and it likes to grab external objects from all directions. Some people's mind is too coarse, so when they try to collect inwardly, wandering thoughts appear very strongly and their mind is very active. This disperses the strength for concentration. Hence, to see that the "I" we are so attached to is just a composition of causes and conditions, we must see it through the actual experience of our own body and mind.

Impermanent Self

When we observe wandering thoughts in practice, many things that have happened in the past come to the surface. Seen from the viewpoint of impermanence, they have obviously passed away. That we store them in our mind is based on the view of permanence and connects past, present, and future. If we view them from the vantage point of impermanence, investigating things of the past, the past causes and conditions, and the time element of the past, we will discover that causes and conditions constantly change — things have already passed and no longer exist with the arising and ceasing of past causes and conditions. The reason we continue to remember them is because what happened has become an image left in our consciousness, forming a karmic force and stored in our mind. They appear in our meditation as retribution. Karma and retribution connect the flow of past, present, and future, thus we see the arising and ceasing in an instant. For example, if we have a certain impression about someone from when they were young, even though in reality they have changed, we believe that they are the never-changing person we knew in the past. Such is the fixed view of permanence.

If you understand impermanence, through the arising and ceasing of wandering thoughts, you can see the operation of your own body and mind, as well as your own thoughts and breaths. We are so accustomed to our breathing that we think every breath is the same. Counting from one to ten, one round after another, are the breaths the same? If you observe carefully, they are not. Usually our mind is not sufficiently refined in order to notice the changes. We only observe their arising and ceasing, and these are not the same either. Even though we are unable to perceive the subtle differences, we can nonetheless see the coarse form of differences, and this tells us that they are changing all the time. Through the practice of observation, it is easier to perceive the phenomenon of impermanence.

When you have a good understanding about the teaching of impermanence and use it in observing what happened in the past, you can slowly let go of the past and need not continue carrying the memories. If they appear in sitting, it means this karmic force has not been extinguished and is still hidden in your consciousness. But do not worry — continue to illuminate your mind with the principle of impermanence. After these are extinguished, do not let them arise again. In the beginning, our wisdom about impermanence may not be sufficient to keep this from happening, but it can help lessen the impact of afflictions. As wisdom increases, as soon as afflictions arise, use the teaching of impermanence to shed light on it and afflictions can be cut off. If the last deluded thought is extinguished from our mind and the recycle has ended, our problem is solved.

We need to be able to contemplate the arising and ceasing of phenomena so clearly that we can perceive the truth of no-self from impermanence. Only after seeing the truth of no-self, can we see the operation of impermanence. No-self means that all phenomena, including those of this world and those of the supramundane, are devoid of self. We need to contemplate this from the actual phenomena, which is to observe this false self and see what this no- self is made of. Through such investigation, we can see clearly that the false self is the composition of the causes and conditions and it is impermanent.

There is absolutely nothing in the world that is solid and constant, nor is there any individual entity which does not change. Can scientists in Physics really measure the minutest unit? No. The micro objects being that are talked about in Buddhism are the same concept. In the end, the analysis of any object cannot demonstrate a constant self-existing unit. All phenomena are like this. We are unable to see such a micro thing. We should understand this not only from theory but also from our own body and mind. Is the life of a human being a form of composition? It is indeed.

Investigating Self

The "I" as we view it has several aspects. One of them is that it does not change; another is that it exists independently, having a solid body which can be completely controlled. However, to analyze these characteristics in our individual life, can we find any of them that are eternal and never change? Can we find any part that exists independently? It is impossible. If "I" were an entity, the entity should have a main body, correct? But which part of the body is the entity? Which function of the mind is the entity? As we reflect on this, if there is an "I", is the one which has the leg pain the "I" or the one which does not have leg pain? If the one with the leg pain is "I", then I would always have leg pain! If the one who does not have leg pain were "I", then would I never have leg pain? Which part of the body is "I"? Is it the heart? If the stomach or intestines were the "I", we can then remove the heart and lungs and only keep the stomach and intestines. Is that correct?

From observing our own body and mind we see that this individual life is only a form with many cells and organs. The deeper operation is of the mind which includes the spirit. Over a long period of time, what we have learned is mixed into our consciousness. When wandering thoughts operate, which one is "I"? When we sit, memory of what happened when we were thirty years old comes up. Is the thirty year old the "I"? No. I am forty years old now, so that is not the "I". If it were, it would mean that when I was born, I was forty years old, and it would be impossible for me to have been born then. If it were "I", I would not need to be born of my parents. This tells us that what we think is the "I" is not real. This individual life, having its mind functioning, makes us feel that there is a real "I". When we break things into pieces and investigate them, we find that it is just a form and that our perception is false, so we can put it down.

Much of our attachments to the self can be put down with such investigation. For instance, sometimes we do not feel well within the body. If we think it is due to various causes and conditions in the ongoing operation or aging process, and that it is normal to have this sort of problem, then we will not suffer because of it. Think again, we might even be grateful when we have such small problems, for then the so-called illness is no longer a cause of suffering.

When something happens that brings us shock or disturbance, it is helpful to ask what is being hurt. If it is the mind being hurt, take it out and put some herbs on it. However, when you want to take the mind out, you cannot find it. Because of clinging to the idea of "I", if you think that someone who is cutting you with a knife is cutting the "I", it would be as if your whole body were being wounded. If you cling to your own opinion and the self, when you recall many things from the past, you will continue to feel hurt. It is like poking a scar to see the wound — it is hurting one again and again. The scar is not a problem since the experience is past, but it is strange that we are so attached to the past and unable to put things down. People have so much suffering because of such accumulations of past wounds. A small thing accumulates, and it becomes a big thing. Small pains continue to accumulate and they become big suffering. This is our mind — strongly attached to the self.

Look at children. Their minds are simple — when things are over, they quickly forget them. When we were young and got injured fighting with other kids, we would just apply some herbs or put a medicinal sticky patch on, and off we would go to play again as if nothing had ever happened. In our minds we did not keep hatred. Without a strong sense of self, we do not store anger. However, as we grow older, we accumulate such emotions as attachments. When one becomes independent from one's parents, the sense of self becomes strong, and self-love also becomes strong. As a result, in growing up, we see our father as "not right"and our mother as "not good". We rebel and we then have all kinds of problems. When we are too self-indulgent, it is very easy to have conflict with others. The stronger the sense of self, the more conflict there is with others. Because others also have attachments to the self, there is collision.

As we continue to investigate the making of our body and mind, slowly we understand the concept of no-self, which is the core teaching of Buddhism. When we study the Heart Sutra, we need to first be clear about the law of the five elements. This law completely explains the formation and process of life — the functions of the body, the functions of mind, feelings, volition, action, and perception. Then we understand how the twelve stations and the eighteen realms operate which explains how sentient beings and life are formed. With such investigation, we understand that life is a process of cyclic phenomena in which there is the law of dependent origination. Also, all phenomena are relative — if there is arising, there must be a ceasing. So, seeing dependent origination from the other end, we see the cessation of it. This is a constant changing process, an inevitable function of dependent origination. If it is so, returning to our self or anything and seeing its nature, knowing everything is such a composition and also constantly changing, this demonstrates that there is no unchanging entity that exists. It is like disassembling something — you cannot find a center or substance, it is only consisting of many parts. Therefore we say the nature of all phenomena is empty, the nature of life that is consisting of the five elements is empty, and only when the five elements are combined, does a form of life appear.

If we can see that the five elements are without a self, knowing that the nature of life is no-self, and actually realizing this core of the Buddhist teachings, it is liberation. The cyclic flow or samsara still continues because of our wrong view and attachment to the self, thinking that there is an entity as the center that really exists. With this imaginary center, there is self-clinging and the sense of self is really strong. The clinging in intellect is ignorance; in feelings, it is self-love. With all of our daily life operating around this center, it becomes sustained. If we find that this center is actually empty, then nothing will have a place to stick. Once the self and the attachment to the self are broken through, all the afflictions that we think exist will also have no place to stick because there is no function at the center. The reason we feel that the self really exists is because we cling to the functions of self. Our sense faculties and perceptions lead us to this mistaken view. Breaking through self-attachment is the result of practice.

Through investigation and reflection, we learn to truly comprehend the teaching of no-self and then to use it to break our attachment. If we can break such an attachment in our mind, the view that caused us to cling to the false self breaks and we let it go. In the beginning of Chan practice, since we are unable to perceive this false center, we can only investigate by brushing off layers of afflictions. As soon as we cut through certain afflictions and enter inside, all surrounding parts will naturally collapse and dissolve. Sometimes we only cut through and dissolve the inner part so that it does not continue its cycle, but if the parts are not yet completely dissolved, their operation will still remain. Hence, Bodhisattvas who appear in various forms or those enlightened beings who are still in this form of body still have karmic retributions. This karmic retribution is to clear out past karma, not to create new karma because, without this entity of self, the root has been extinguished.

If we can further recognize that not only the individual life consisting of the five elements has no-self but also that each element is a composition and there is no element which exists as self or unchanging, such investigation is more thorough and the self will no longer hold fast. It is like a fist with its five fingers closed. As soon as it is opened, it changes and is a "palm" and no longer a fist. Furthermore, each finger is not seen as that solid either. If every finger is cut off, there is nothing. The no-self referred to in Mahayana Buddhism is like this — not only that the body and mind are empty, but also that the five elements are empty. Each and every element is empty. Thus the Heart Sutra says, "Form is no different from emptiness, emptiness is no different from form. Form is emptiness, emptiness is form." The scripture also says, "feelings, volitions, perceptions are the same", which means that each element is no different than emptiness. Then there is the negation of eye, ear, nose, tongue, body and perception — each and every thing is negated. Negation does not mean that the five elements do not exist, but rather that their nature is empty. Empty nature means there is no "I" in the five elements. It is constantly combining and changing. When causes and conditions meet, form, feelings, volitions, and perception will appear, and the physical body still exists.

From the nature of life, if we can see no-self, which is emptiness, we will not cling to the individual life form, nor to its mind and consciousness. In practice, we are doing precisely this, which is to truly understand the Dharma through layers after layers of worldly phenomena. Through observation we realize the true nature of all dharmas.

Realizing No-Self

Although we know no-self to be the core of the teaching, and we continue to contemplate no-self, it does not always feel intimate or directly relevant to us. Only after having realized it through experience will we feel that the theory and the actual are connected. When we have only studied the Dharma but have not directly experienced its teaching, there remains a gap between theory and practice. This is partly due to the lack of depth in understanding. Sometimes it is because the mind is not stable enough to be able to concentrate, and there are too many wandering thoughts pulling away our attention. We need to slowly adjust these areas of insufficiency.

When practice goes well, theory and experience will be more or less in sync. When one has not reached realization or enlightenment and still feels the need to think of the theory of no-self in order to penetrate, this means that the state of no hindrance between intellect and experience has not been reached. Otherwise, there would be no hindrance in contemplation of any phenomena — in every contact with the object, no ignorance manifests.

At the moment of contact, if our perception and experience are not two but one with no-hindrance, the mind is naturally empty. This function of knowing works when causes and conditions are met which is in itself also no-self and empty. With this state of no-hindrance, as events happen, one can know the nature of dependent origination and can see that causes and conditions have met and, at the same time know the nature of it is empty — not two things but totally unified. Because of that, the mind will naturally follow the causes and conditions in the moment.

The instant causes and conditions meet is the present moment, and it very rapidly arises and ceases. If one can be completely in harmony with that moment, it is living in the present. The before and after that connect the two are just the function of cause, and because their nature is empty, consciousness will not continue the function of cycling them. Awareness connects them and forms a knowledge or opinion. In this process we often add a cyclic driving force due to ignorance and clinging. With wisdom, if theory and experience are unified, it will not have such function.

When no-self is realized, it does not mean that this person no longer exists nor operates. Mind consciousness is kept. In the Consciousness-Only School, "eight consciousnesses" become four types of wisdom which actually are the function of perception. Perception contains stains and can recycle with birth and death. Wisdom has cleansed the stains. The function of wisdom and consciousness are the same, however wisdom does not have impurity. Thus when one has realized no-self, the person still lives well, and their mind and body are not dissolved; rather, wisdom is aware of everything. It is different from the conventional sense of consciousness in which these are distinguished in nature — one is stained, the other is pure. It is not that, when one is enlightened, one will be seeing with the mouth — it is still the eyes that are seeing; it is just that with the eyes looking without impurity, the sixth, the seventh, and the eighth consciousness are all connected — awareness has no discrimination.

Often when things happen, we quickly react. Is such reaction pure or stained? Or is it more stained and less pure? This is related to one's practice. The more cultivated one is, when there is a reaction in consciousness, it is more likely to be in accord with the Dharma and less with cyclic force. Usually there are impure or covered ingredients in people's reactions which are added thinking or strategizing. For instance, at the time of a car accident, what are our reactions? It is a most direct reaction and will be a reflection of our level of cultivation. We have heard the story about a time when Venerable Master Yin Shun was riding in a car that someone crashed into. Everyone in the car hurriedly jumped out, leaving only Master Yin Shun sitting peacefully inside. They said his samadhi was very deep. Actually it was his wisdom that was deep — in that instant he had seen through birth and death. To him, birth and death were not something separate, so that when things happen, he could respond without panic.

Another situation that can reveal one's cultivation is when death comes. If someday you feel ill and your doctor suddenly says to you, "Wherever you wish to travel, go as you please. Whatever you love to eat, eat as you please." What will your reaction be? If you ask the doctor how many months you have left and the answer is "two", and you figure out what can be done in that time and simply try to finish it, this means that you have truly seen through birth and death and know no-self.

So if one cultivates well, their reactions will be in accord with Dharma, and their actions will follow the teachings of the Dharma. If there is too much impurity, one's reactions will be full of affliction. If one only tries to look as though one has cultivated well, before long the truth will be revealed. Having understood this, in practice and daily life, try not to cover things up — there is no need to decorate your cultivation. If you can verify no-self by seeing it through your life, theory and experience will become closer. When the one who observes and the object of observation are unified, because their nature is empty and only in function they seem to be separated, it makes everything relative. Thus, in contemplating no-self, if one perceives the object as empty, on returning to contemplate the function of observing, one can see it is also empty because the function of observing is based on the object.

There can be situations where, in sitting meditation, when the sense faculty of eye looks at an object, the object is being observed and the eye is the function of seeing. In contemplation, one may feel the two become closer. Practice is the same way — we will get closer and closer to no-self; theory and experience will also become closer. Finally they are unified and are without hindrance. Then, the so-called state of enlightenment will manifest and function. When this state is actually operating, the mind is very clearly sees theory and experience as unified. Then, one will find the nature of all sentient beings, even external things, is empty.

Why do bodhisattvas in practice have the so-called "great compassion which treat everything as if it is their own?" Because all beings are actually one and the nature is empty. This is the emptiness the Dharma talks about. It is different from the entity talked about in philosophy. In Daoism, they say "The Dao creates one, one creates two, two creates three, and three creates ten thousand (myriad) things", and "the Dao is the original nature." They believe that there is an origin and then things are created from that. But Buddhism does not talk about that. From the Buddhist perspective, everything that exists at the moment, from things as big as the universe to the smallest particle, are one and empty in nature. But because the forms of the different phenomenon are individual and because everything appears to have form and function, in recognizing them, our mind discriminates and creates illusions.

However, no matter how they are seemingly opposed to each other, their original nature is empty. All phenomena that we can be conscious of, theory and phenomena included, all just appear to have a form, which is dependent on emptiness. In other words, all dharma or phenomena have the nature of emptiness and no-self. When one has realized enlightenment, it is the mind enlightened to true nature, which we call "Buddha-nature". Therefore the nature of Dharma and Buddha are not two.

Regardless of Dharma-nature or Buddha-nature, if they are empty, there is absolutely no impurity. What can stain emptiness? Nothing. So empty nature must be pure. This is the concept of purity in Buddhism. All sentient beings are endowed with Buddha-nature. Because this is one's nature, one does not need to look elsewhere. As long as we use awareness and through practice thoroughly understand this nature and let the function of emptiness and purity manifest, it is enlightenment which is the manifestation of Buddha-nature.

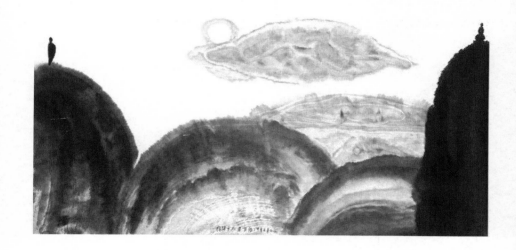

8

From East to the West

So far we have been looking at the common issues people often encounter in Chan practice and the approaches for dealing with them. As background, we will now take a historical view of the development of Buddhism and Chinese Chan, giving you some perspective from which to understand the method of huatou in the Chinese Chan tradition, which will be highlighted in the next chapter.

The Development of Buddhism

After the Buddha was enlightened, in the environment of India at that time, through practice, he adapted some ideas in Indian philosophy and began to teach what he had realized. Upon hearing his teachings, many people understood and followed him. Afterwards, they spread the Dharma based on their own understandings and realization.

India has religion and philosophy at the heart of its culture, and its content is very rich. Many of Buddha's disciples had some form of practice before they began following the Buddha, and some of them even had experiences of very deep states of samadhi. The Buddha only pointed them to the key principles, and immediately they were enlightened. This is saying that, in their understanding of philosophy, they already had knowledge about the causes and conditions of the cycle of birth and death. Thus, as soon as they heard the Buddha's teaching about the doctrine of dependent origination and no-self, they quickly realized the truth.

Nowadays, it is also not so very difficult for those who are highly educated in science to study Buddhism. It is not necessary for them to study the terms or concepts of the five elements, the twelve stations, the eighteen realms, etc. because they can understand these through the disciplines of their own academic studies. What is lacking is a way for them to connect all of their own studies of the theories of the Dharma into a core understanding. Therefore, upon hearing the teaching of dependent origination, they can immediately put together all of their knowledge and understand the principle of no-self. All of their questioning can just naturally fall away.

It seems that in the process of its development, every culture keeps reaching one peak after another. Other cultures are like this, and Chinese culture is the same. Chinese culture reached its highest peak during the time of Confucianism, and the entire nation was deeply impacted by this philosophy. Whether it was fully accepted or not, it had a significant influence on people's thinking. The same was true of India. When religion in India reached its highest peak, Buddhism emerged and then widely spread. Later in its reform, Hinduism adapted some aspects from Buddhism. In the revolution of Brahmanism to become Hinduism, Śavkara also applied many aspects of popular philosophy from Buddhism, including the thoughts of Nāgārjuna. Therefore, even though later Buddhism became extinct in India, its thoughts and ideology still exist in the Indian philosophy of religion.

Buddhism was introduced from India to China during the late years of the Han Dynasty (206BCE-220CE) through the era of the Northern and Southern Dynasties (420-589). In about seven or eight hundred years or until the Tang Dynasty (618-907), Chinese culture was brought to its second peak after Confucianism. From that time on, the spreading of culture definitely manifested the influence of Buddhism. Even today in China, the concept of "three periods of cause-and-effect" is well known to the general population. The word commonly used in daily chats, "affinity" (yuan, causes and conditions) appeared after Buddhism came to China. Even the Neo-

Confucianism of the Song (960-1279) and Ming (1368-1644) Dynasties evolved out of combined aspects of philosophy from Chan or Buddhism. Thus, regardless of whether non-Buddhists of today wish to accept Buddhism or not, Buddhist ideas have had an affect on many cultures and societies throughout the world.

In order to spread the Dharma, Buddhist sects also adopted some non-Buddhist ideas which is one of the reasons there were various reforms in different Buddhist sects. What does not change and is consistent in all Buddhist sects however, are the doctrines of dependent origination and no-self. Thus we see that the southern lineage of Theravada and the northern lineage of Chinese Buddhism, both preach the teaching of dependent origination and no-self — only the depth or approach may be different.

In the Theravada system of thought, although the Buddha and the eminent disciples have many things in common — for example, they are all arhats — the meritorious virtue of the Buddha is seen to be higher than that of the disciples, and there can be only one Buddha. When Mahayana Buddhism was developed from the early tradition of Buddhism, there emerged the concept of Buddha-nature, which believes that all beings have awakened nature, and through practice, every being eventually can achieve Buddhahood. After this concept that "all beings have Buddha-nature" was brought to China, it was developed even further with the faith that practice or enlightenment itself is "seeing true nature" and becoming a buddha. Seeing what nature? Seeing the Buddha-nature. After the Chan School emerged, it claimed, "This mind is Buddha. With this mind one becomes Buddha." In other words, seeing the Buddha-nature is becoming a buddha. The Chan sect thus emphasizes "cultivating the mind and seeing true nature." When one realizes this mind of perceiving true nature, it is enlightenment, which is buddha, the awakened one. An even more popular concept was, "one enlightened thought is one thought of buddha." This one enlightened thought is not complete enlightenment, but at the instant of seeing emptiness as the nature of all phenomena, this one thought in such an instant is buddha. If every thought is enlightened thought, then every thought is buddha. This is the brilliance of the Chan sect which points out that one can see Buddha-nature from this body and mind. Furthermore, the Chan School teaches that becoming a buddha is not enough. And as some patriarchs said, "What is Buddha? — Not only must you see the Buddha-nature; you have to surpass the Buddha." This is brilliant. Those who claimed this were not just daring to say so — the patriarchs who said this spoke from actual realization. This was also a way of countering those who lacked confidence in the idea that "All beings are endowed with Buddha-nature." If we say these words now, we must evaluate our ability and see how much reality there is to it. When those Chan masters spoke these words, the confidence in them was very firm. Regardless of what methods they used, the patriarchs were sincere and they firmly believed that they were a buddha and that what they did was all from the immaculate mind.

In the development of Buddhism in China, Tiantai and Huayen were the schools that blended Chinese culture in their teaching systems. At that time, Buddhism was very widely spread throughout the society. Even the entry exams to the public offices included tests on the content of Buddhist sutras. We know that the eminent Dharma master, Xuan Zhang, who translated many sutras into Chinese had to take exams to become a Buddhist monk. The popularity of Buddhism at that time meant that most people had knowledge of many concepts about Buddhism; how deep or how shallow was really the question.

The Chan School emerged during the Tang Dynasty, when Buddhism reached its highest peak. It thrived during the time of the Sixth Patriarch, Master Hui Neng. People may wonder, "how did Master Hui Neng, who was illiterate, upon hearing someone recite the Diamond Sutra, understand the teachings?" Actually, Buddhism, at that time, was very popular and knowledge about it was very common.

When Buddhism was introduced to China, most of those who studied it already had a good grasp of Confucian philosophy. For example, the teachings about life in the Agama Sutra or Singalovada Sūtra (a short sutra about ethics and morality) was already in the teachings of Confucianism. So it was unnecessary to teach them; one could talk directly about liberation — the Bodhisattva path.

During that prosperous period, Buddhism was so popular that, many practitioners, as at the time of the Buddha in India, upon hearing a few sentences of Dharma discourse in the Chan hall or hit by the incense board from the master, became enlightened. Do not imagine that they did not have the firm foundation of Buddhism — they had already understood the principles of Chinese philosophy or Buddhism. In particular, those disciples who began their practice in forest-dwelling Chan communities were from all parts of the country, and many of them had studied Buddhism before they traveled and studied with the great Chan masters.

An example is Chan Master Dan Xian who was originally a bright scholar. On his way to the city to take the qualification exam for government positions, someone said to him, "to be selected to be a scholar is inferior to being selected to be buddha." What is being selected as buddha? — It is enlightenment. Upon hearing this, he gave up the exam and became a monk to practice Chan. Without the foundation in Buddhism that he had, it would have been inconceivable to do what he did in choosing the enlightened path. You have probably heard the story about an old lady who, with only a few words about the Diamond Sutra, deflated a well-versed scholar monk. If Buddhadharma were not so popular, how would an ordinary woman who sells cakes in a sweet shop understand the teachings of the Diamond Sutra? This tells us that in the Tang Dynasty, Buddhism was very widely known.

From the methods that the Chan sect employed, we can see that some masters did not teach about the doctrines. Instead, they helped their disciples to directly penetrate the mind. The cases of gong-an (koan) recorded such teaching dialogues between masters and disciples, either verifying a student's enlightenment or not confirming their experiences of realization. There is not much written about the teaching of the doctrines because most practitioners already knew the theory.

In the later period of development of Buddhism, there appeared a gap during which the link with the local Chinese culture was lost. In modern society, saying that there is no Buddhist thoughts in people's minds would be inaccurate, for even though our knowledge is incomplete, most people know a little bit. People can speak fluently about science because it permeates the culture. Science has spread throughout western civilization as this culture has reached its peak. Much of the knowledge that is available is about science, and it seems easy for people to learn and understand. If this knowledge cannot connect one with the Buddhadharma, when they study Buddhism, one has to start from the beginning, utilizing the complete system of Buddhist teaching. However, there are well-cultivated scholars in the field of science who are able to organize and summarize the principles that connect with the Dharma. The more advanced the science is, the closer are its ideas and views to the Buddhist view.

At the time of the Buddha, knowledge was expressed through the wisdom of religion and philosophy. Today, knowledge is expressed through science. These approaches are different, but knowledge in science is helpful in the studying of Buddhism. In other words, from what we learn in general, we can see the Dharma. Why? Because what the Dharma explains is about the characteristics of all dharma and the laws of their operation. With such an understanding, going deeply into the essence of any field of study will gradually lead towards the principles of the Dharma.

Characteristics of Chinese Chan

The development of Chinese Chan reflected its favor of simplification in Chinese culture. With the belief that all beings have Buddha-nature which is originally pure and immaculate, Chan masters put down many other details of the teachings in Buddhism and directly pointed the students to the mind of the matter — the true nature of all phenomena. Most practitioners at that time had basic knowledge about Buddhism and a very firm confidence that they had Buddha-nature and could be enlightened. What did they have confidence in? They believed they could become a Buddha and could surpass the Buddha. They aimed for this and made great effort in their practice. They also had the great desire to solve the problem of birth and death. If one does not feel birth and death are suffering and want to be liberated from suffering, how much power does one have in practice? It might be the case that, as soon as there is a leg pain, all of one's power is gone. Why? It is probably because one does not feel liberation to be more important or urgent than the leg pain. If they did, would the leg pain matter? With great determination and good preparation, regardless of what methods the masters use in teaching, the students are able to be diligent and to practice deeply.

Actually during the time that the Chan School was flourishing, there was no fixed method of teaching — great Chan masters had their own approaches for guiding their disciples based on the students' karmic tendencies and personalities. The styles they utilized were developed based on their own practice and personality. Many Chan masters in the Tang Dynasty had great vision and wisdom, and they used various approaches to train their disciples. If you read the Platform Sutra by the Sixth Patriarch, Master Hui Neng, it is not difficult to see how lively the teachings were at that time — very directly and vigorously engaging with the students to help them transform their impediments. For instance, a master giving one disciple a torch, and then suddenly having the torch set to explode, or the case of a master pushing a disciple through a doorway and rapidly closing a door in such a way that the fellow ended up with a broken foot. In other words, as long as these masters facilitated an enlightenment experience, it did not matter what method they used. Later these various styles of the Chan masters were utilized in the teachings of their disciples.

With great Chan masters teaching like that, if one is in accord with it, very quickly one can achieve the state of awakening. For instance, Chan Master Bai Zhang, knowing that one of his disciples was very well versed in the sutras, said to the disciple when this disciple asked for his teachings, "You have studied the sutras so thoroughly — let me ask you a question. What was your original face before you were born?" The disciple heard this and went to look for an answer in the texts. He could not find any mention of it. He went to ask his master for the correct answer. Master Bai Zhang said, "If I told you the answer, it would not be yours." The disciple then threw away all his books and traveled about without speaking of anything. What do you think he was doing? He was practicing diligently. How did he practice? He was investigating "what is your original face before you were born?" What is it? — it is Buddha-nature. But as soon as one speaks about it, it is thinking, and it is not realization. So he kept his practice like that until one day, as he was doing some physical work, unintentionally throwing a rock, he heard the sound of the rock hitting the bamboo, and he suddenly realized the teaching and had an enlightenment experience. Immediately he prostrated toward the direction where his master was, thanking him for not telling him the answer.

In the Song Dynasty, when the strength of the Chan sect was gradually diminishing, the daring and free style of Chan teaching did not develop as it did in Tang Dynasty. Instead, some masters used more fixed forms to teach their disciples. The most well-known masters of the time were Master Dai-Hui Zong-Gao in the Linji (Rinzai) tradition, who developed the format of using huatou (a question or short phrase), and Master Hong-Zhi Zheng-Jue in the Caodong (Soto) sect, who used the so-called "silent illumination" method in teaching his disciples.

Later in Ming Dynasty, Chan Master Jie Xian of Hui Shan wrote a volume called Talks on Training in Chan. It described how Chan masters used to train their disciples. Some of the methods were very forceful and were for the purpose of meeting the particular needs of some disciples. Nowadays, practitioners usually do not have a karmic capacity to receive this type of training. Also, if these methods were to be used, they would have to be used in appropriately suitable training temples. It is possible that in Linji temples these days, even though they might follow the tradition of monastic forest-dwelling, that no one — not even the abbot of the temple — would know how to use the actual Linji method. In Japan and Korea, there are still some temples where traditional methods are used and transmission of the mind is continued.

I myself learned Chan from Master Sheng Yen. He himself did use the traditional method of Chinese Chan, particularly silent illumination, in his personal solitary retreat. The period when his practice really took off, though, was when he was in Japan. While he was in school for Buddhist academic study in Japan, he took training with Master Ban Tetsugyu Soin (Hanamaki), a disciple of Master Harada Daiun Sogaku. His profound experience in practice was confirmed (given inka) after a seven-day retreat. Master Sheng Yen's teaching is not completely traditional since his lineage is from Master Dong Chu, who was a descendent of Caodong (Soto) tradition. After returning to Taiwan, Master Sheng Yen also received transmission from Master Ling Yuan, who was the second generation of Master Xu Yun (known as Empty Cloud) from the lineage of Linji. Master Sheng Yen's teaching is profound in its width and depth, and the Chan teaching he has transmitted is very systematic and deeply rooted in Chinese Chan.

Chan Beyond China

Influenced by Chinese culture, Korean Seon and Japanese Zen, variants of Chinese Chan, share the common trait of paying attention to the preservation of their traditions. They do very well in this regard. If you go to Japan, you can still see the Tang Dynasty style of architecture which is hard to find in China. Many temples in China were rebuilt during the Ming dynasty. In Japan, even the rebuilt temples maintain the original Chinese style. In Korea there are similar temples. We also know that tea ceremony in Japan was introduced from the Tang and Song eras of China, and was moderated to suit Japanese folk culture.

The Korean or Japanese Chan masters do only one thing in their life. They teach Chan, and they do a great job in this regard. Their teaching is also very organized and has a clear lineage which was transmitted from generation to generation. The Jogye tradition of Korean Seon is very similar to the Chan from the Tang Dynasty in China, which is penetrating one thought, though not using the method of huatou since the formal use of huatou did not appear in China until the Song Dynasty, and Chinese Buddhism spread to Korea before that. Japanese Zen uses the method of huatou, which was transmitted to Japan in the Song era. In temples of the Rinzai (Linji) tradition, for example, they investigate the koan (huatou) "What is wu?" Now the teaching of Chan is developing in the West.

At the time of the Buddha, the Buddha could use any approach he saw fit in his teaching. After his paranirvana, his disciples were divided into different sects as their teaching styles slowly formalized. From the emerging of Mahayana Buddhism to the spread of Chinese Chan, many styles have since been developed. This is why we can see multitudinous varieties of styles of Buddhist teachings in the world, each playing its particular role according to the causes and conditions in a given environment.

In the West, the teaching of meditation is gaining much attention these days. Particularly in America, there are more and more people who are interested in learning meditation. People are learning from the Theravada tradition such as Wisdom Meditation of Burma, Insight Meditation taught by Goenka, and also from other esoteric traditions of Buddhism. Japanese

Zen came to America earlier through its introduction by D. T. Suzuki, the eminent scholar. His many books on Zen were very popular although he himself seldom taught meditation. Also Korean Zen was brought to America by Master Seung Sahn in the early 1970's.

Master Sheng Yen was the master who taught Chinese Chan in the United States. However, the mindset of American practitioners is quite different from that of the Chinese. Many of them are mainly interested in meditation but not so much in the doctrines. Their main motivation seems to be to have an enlightenment experience or for stress reduction purposes since stress seems to be such a major problem in western culture. Jack Kornfield, the author of A Path With Heart, upon returning from Thailand after several years of being a monk, went into to the field of psychology and used meditation to help his patients in this way. Many Americans learn meditation just wanting to reduce some psychological pressure. Sometimes they continue the practice because they feel meditation to be helpful — maybe more so in some instances than psychotherapy.

We can see that the adoption of Buddhism in the West has similarity to the situation in China — a highly developed civilization, when adopting something from a foreign culture, does not accept everything in its entirety. As Buddhism spread to China, teachers used their own methods, which is how sects such as Chan emerged. Chinese Chan is different from the Indian tradition or Theravada tradition — it has Chinese characteristics as we mentioned earlier in this chapter. Buddhism in America is experiencing a somewhat similar process. First, meditation as a technique is absorbed from the different traditions and slowly the doctrines are found to be important because all meditation methods must have a theoretical foundation. Without a firm theoretical foundation, meditation is more or less just stress reduction or mental healing and lacks an ultimate aim. This is the reason practitioners need to study the doctrine. In this area, Chinese Chan can play a paramount role. However, Chinese Chan is still rather new in America, mostly taught by Master Sheng Yen.

From the viewpoint of Chinese Chan, the methods of practice that people learn cannot rely completely on the traditions of another culture but must evolve and be redesigned according to the needs of the local population. The teaching system of Chinese Chan itself still needs improvement. Although studying it sometimes feels challenging, hopefully a more comprehensive system that is clearer and more complete can be gradually developed. In order to revive Chinese Chan and help it to once more become fully alive, more time and great effort of practice will be needed.

9

Huatou – Before Words

With the overview in the previous chapter on Chinese Chan from a historical perspective, we have some understanding about the social and cultural conditions in which Chan emerged and flourished in China, its central belief on one's Buddha-nature, its lively teaching style of "directly pointing to the mind," and the use of huatou in practice. Now, without going into technical details of the method, we will highlight some aspects of huatou practice – the investigation into what is before words.

Confidence is the Key

Probably you are familiar with the story about the famous dialog between Bodhidharma, who was credited with transmitting Chan to China and was regarded as the first Patriarch of its lineage, and Huike, who became the second Patriarch. Huike approached Bodhidharma outside the cave where Bodhidharma had been meditating for years and asked him for his teachings, "Venerable Master, my mind is unsettled, please help me settle it." Bodhidharma replied, "Well, give me your mind, I'll settle it for you." Huike looked and said, "But I cannot find my mind." Bodhidharma replied, "I have settled it then." Upon hearing this, Huike was enlightened – There is no mind, what is there to settle? Problem solved! Such an encounter is a classic illustration of the teaching style of Chinese Chan – pointing directly to the mind and seeing Buddha-nature. Later in Song Dynasty, this direct approach was further formulated into the method of huatou, a question usually given by a master to a disciple in order to go deeply inward and investigate. It was widely used in Chan School, especially in the Linji sect.

Huatou is used to help point directly to the mind; therefore it must be very simple, such as "What is wu?" or "What was my original face before I was born?" or more direct investigation of "Who am I?" Such types of questions help the practitioner to first let go of all wandering thoughts. So usually in the beginning, the practice is to simply recite the huatou. As the huatou arises in the mind, one keeps asking. Slowly the questioning becomes stronger and more intense. The phrase "water can not pour through" describes this condition of mind when even wandering thoughts cannot break the continuity of huatou inquiry. Gradually the sense of questioning or doubt is condensed to a force, which is often referred as the "great doubt" or the "mass of doubt."

For the huatou method to work, the practitioner must have great confidence. What confidence? It is the knowing that one can realize in one's mind and see the true nature of all phenomena. This confidence is grounded in deep understanding of the Buddhadharma. With the firm belief that one has Buddha-nature and the sense of great doubt, and with practice, one can breakthrough delusive thinking and perceive true nature. True nature means the nature of all dharma or phenomena is originally pure and immaculate. When the mind can penetrate this, it sees Buddha-nature. At this time one is said to have an experience of enlightenment.

Investigating huatou is actually a type of contemplation, although it is a little different from the traditional approach. Traditional contemplation is through understanding of the Dharma and establishing right view. If one can grasp well the principle of emptiness and contemplate, having theory and actual experience mutually verify each other, then wisdom naturally manifests. Having penetrated the mind, one can reach the state of no-hindrance and unification, at which time one is said to have realized and entered the Dharma realm. This contemplation of Dharma nature, after seeing it is empty, returns to contemplating the one who is doing the contemplation. Here one finds that it is also empty and all, including the one who contemplates, is relative existence based on causes and conditions. If you only see the objects of contemplation as empty, it is merely analysis, not true contemplation. Doing a practice process like this will have the effects of purifying one's mind, even if one is unable to achieve the state of enlightenment. As one studies the Dharma, it purifies the mind. Indian Buddhism very much emphasizes studying the doctrines, and each sect has a complete system of teaching. The treatises compiled by the Theravada tradition also have their own complete doctrine for studying.

The practice of huatou is similar to the "returning" method of contemplation as described in The Six Gates to the Sublime of the Tiantai classic text. If you know that method, practicing huatou is relatively easy. In keeping at "returning" and going inward in contemplation, huatou helps to penetrate to the core of self. In traditional practice of contemplation, as one continues in observing the object of contemplation, one will find that behind the object there is no one who is observing. It is same with investigating huatou. In investigating the huatou, one is not going outward but inward to where the thought of the huatou has not arisen; this is prior to words. Hence in practice, if thoughts appear, the huatou immediately enters so all wandering thoughts are cut off with no chance to arise. Then one keeps going inwardly and investigates. If one goes outward in asking the question of huatou, there is no power to penetrate the mind. If many of the coarse wandering thoughts are cleared up through practice and one is able to collect the mind, investigating huatou can be powerful.

Great Doubt is Essential

Huatou practice is a rather fierce method, requiring quite a bit of strength in applying it. In investigating huatou, one must have doubt. Without it, it is merely reciting the words. Is it useful to merely recite the huatou? There are some benefits. One of them is, after reciting it for a long time, the sense of doubt might arise. Some people in the beginning only recite it, using the method to cultivate stillness and awareness. If one cannot raise the sensation of doubt, just continue to recite until concentration and awareness are unified.

When reciting it, clearly know that you are reciting the huatou and keep only the huatou in your mind; then wandering thoughts will fall away and become less active. In some cases, reciting the huatou in a very concentrated manner with awareness at all times can produce a certain state of samadhi. At such time the huatou can turn into doubt. Investigating huatou is like chewing a vegetable — it becomes more and more tasty, and doubt will slowly cook and arise.

Typically when one studies Buddhism and enters a certain stage of practice, doubt will arise, which is strong curiosity about life. When one wants to know the answer to a question, most people will imagine they have the confidence to find the answer. However, in huatou practice, it is not about finding an answer but clearly knowing that one will find it. Having established such confidence, one simply investigates. In continuously doing so, doubt will arise. This is like exploring the meaning of life — if it has no meaning, how can this be? If it has meaning, then what is it? With knowledge of the method one reflects and further investigates. Eventually the fog of unknowing dissipates and the truth will be clearly seen.

In the beginning of investigating huatou, one might have only a little bit of curiosity, which can be doubt without strength. Continue to investigate and strength will increase and doubt will grow as well. Sometimes the huatou may not seem to raise doubt in you, such as "All dharmas return to one, where does one return?" or "What is wu?" as you simply repeat it. Nonetheless, just keep on asking until you know what it is. This knowing is not a kind of knowledge but rather intimate seeing. In other words, investigating huatou is not getting a "correct" answer. It is only using it to collect the mind and raise the mass of doubt and, in the end, break it. After that, what is it like? — It is breakthrough; it is enlightenment.

Sometimes the huatou given to you by the teacher during the retreat can be useful. Some practitioners just continue to count their breaths until doubt arises in their mind and it becomes a question. A common example is "Who is this I?" or "Who is sitting?" type of huatou. From this type of questioning, one starts to investigate. If the causes and conditions are ripe, when the teacher suddenly throws out a huatou, the student who does well in practice may experience a breakthrough. A good teacher can tell which stage a student is in and gives a push at the right moment. If the student is not ready, it can be merely a waste of energy and there is no impact.

Sometimes practitioners do not experience "great doubt" but somehow causes and conditions enable them to have a breakthrough type of experience. When that happens, it seems powerful. This can be related to the practice of samadhi. With samadhi practice, one feels the object and the one who observes the object becomes closer and closer. So in practice, one can use the method of samadhi and huatou to concentrate. With concentration, when one experiences a breakthrough and their whole being feels a sense of fulfillment, some afflictions and wandering thoughts will fall away. But if they have not developed enough strength in practice, that feeling can quickly vanish. Upon leaving the Chan hall, everything may revert to the condition prior to retreat and the effect of such an experience is not sustained. This is why huatou practice requires being solid in growing "great doubt."

In the later period of Buddhist development in China, the practice of Chan and practice in the Pure Land tradition merged, which combines "mindfulness of the Buddha" or reciting the name of the Buddha with sitting meditation. During the recitation, one may raise the huatou "Who is it that is reciting the name of the Buddha?" However, if you are not mindful of the Buddha in daily life, to investigate this huatou can go nowhere – perhaps there is only the sound of other people's reciting, and it can easily become a formality.

There can be cases where you go to some temples for practice, and you are given a huatou but it does not resonate with you. You may not even be aware but this is the case and you feel your practice is fruitless. This is one of the reasons why in his later years of teaching, Master Sheng Yen assumed a teaching process of beginning from the basics, which is counting the breath, in helping practitioners to first collect their minds and establish stillness as the foundation. After stillness or stability is established, one can then start the practice of contemplation as one does with huatou investigation.

Practice of Huatou

From study we know that, while the faculty of eyes may see objects but has no concept of time, the faculty of mind will link the past, present, and future. The function of huatou disempowers such function so that one can penetrate the mind. As the investigation of the huatou reaches a certain degree of strength, it is described as one entering a so-called "black tank." In this state, practitioners are so concentrated that they may not be able to take care of their daily chores. This is why usually it is not recommended to use huatou method unless one has a qualified teacher to help in the practice. Since this method requires a collection of extreme power internally, investigating till one reaches a state of "seeing the mountain not as a mountain," it is a rather fierce form of practice. It is like blowing up a balloon — if the balloon of mind has holes and leaks, huatou is used to fill them. The leakage is the appearance of wandering thoughts. When all leakages are filled, wandering thoughts cannot arise but the huatou is still going until the balloon explodes.

For example, in Song Dynasty, Chan master Wu-Men Hui-Kai wrote a volume Gateless Gate, in which he mentions gong-an (koan) of the one word "wu" (without). One time someone asked Chan master Zhao Zhou, "Does a dog have Buddha-nature?" Master Zhao Zhou answered, "wu." This word "wu" then became a huatou. Usually people practice with the question "What is wu?" However, Master Zhao Zhou investigated fiercely on the one word "wu", as if taking it as a burning iron ball and put it in mouth — one cannot swallow it, but cannot throw it out either! Investigating huatou is like that. It requires one's whole being concentrated on the investigation without any reservation. With the slightest reservation, when it comes to the critical moment, it will not have the impact of breakthrough.

Another story is about Master Xu Yun (Empty Cloud). He practiced this method and was enlightened when he was over fifty years of age. At that time, he was practicing in a forest monastery, diligently investigating the huatou "Who is it that drags this corpse around?" In the monastery, every afternoon there would be teatime. One day, as the serving person was pouring hot tea into his cup, the tea spilled and burned Master Xu Yun's hands. As his hands suddenly let it go, the cup broke — Bam! The empty sky shattered and in that moment he saw the true nature of all phenomena.

In modern time, we can still use the method of investigating huatou. If there were ideal temples, one could live there and do such training, concentrating on the huatou. However, there is a lack of ideal training temples nowadays. Thus we seldom see teachings with such traditional method of Chinese Chan.

10

The Path of Living Wisdom

During my teaching tours in the United States I met many scholars, some of whom even have several doctorate degrees. For some, participating in Buddhist study seems, especially in the beginning, like going to a social event, because a Buddhist group is often a connection with other like-minded people. Some of these people come to hear Dharma talks as an intellectual pursuit. Some of them, due to ripening of causes and conditions, are interested in the practice and quickly become involved in serious study. In discussions with them I noticed that the core of Buddhist teachings often stimulate their thinking. One time, a person with a doctorate in Physics and I were chatting about the topic of "multiple space". Another person joined the conversation and said, "The space of the mind of those enlightened practitioners is perhaps twenty dimensional!" Perhaps because research in physics has thus far only involved ten dimensions, they think it must take many more dimensions to express the state of mind of the Buddha or bodhisattvas. I said to them, "It should be zero dimensional." They had never thought of that, and their interest was aroused. The so-called space of zero-dimension is actually empty, and the principle of emptiness is the core of Mahayana Buddhism. Only zero can be without limit — everything else comes from zero or nothing. From the point view of Buddhism, such space of zero-dimension does not exist in the domain of physics. Hence when I mentioned this, that particular scholar became very enthused and we continued talking about this subject. In the past he would probably not have been very keen to study the doctrines of Buddhism, but this incident aroused his curiosity and encouraged him to explore more deeply.

Your Own Path

In the reading of Buddhist classics, while some people may feel intimately connected to the teaching, others, even if they have read Buddhist texts for many years, have not experienced Dharma penetration. Perhaps, in many cases, being able to quickly digest the learning of Dharma is like harvesting the fruits when they have ripened – people had planted the seeds and put much effort into their study in the past. At the beginning of the study, we are all planting seeds of the Dharma. Slowly the fruits will grow and, when ripe, they will fall onto the ground, which is liberation. In the process, some people may have reached the ripened stage, and they seem to be ahead of the game. Do not doubt appearances since they absolutely follow the law of cause and effect – how much effort we put in and how much wholesome karma we have generated in the past is how much fruit it will produce. The law of cause and effect cannot be mistaken. If it were, whose mistake would it be? It is we who made mistakes – the law of cause and effect will not make mistakes.

Some people, upon hearing the Dharma and finding resonance within, naturally take the teachings to heart, apply them in daily practice, and very quickly become involved on the bodhisattva path. There are others who, with a simple heart of kindness, are already active in charity works prior to studying Buddhism. Regardless of the manner in which each comes to the practice, the causes and conditions of each individual are different. The same holds true for the learning of meditation. Some people can quickly apply a method because of their karmic conditions. Perhaps due to the fact that their minds are simple with less afflictions, they are able to concentrate and work with the methods easily. If we believe in the law of cause and effect, we will honestly practice according to our own karmic condition. If we experience too much affliction or our wandering thoughts are overly chaotic, it is a fact and we must accept it. We must employ suitable methods to help adjust our life, reducing unwholesome actions and keeping the cultivation of wholesome karma as the root.

It is important to keep in mind that, in learning and practicing the Chan method, one needs to understand the essentials of Buddhadharma. Chan practice is based on the principles that dharma nature is empty and that our Buddha-nature is immaculate. In the beginning, from the external to the internal, we cleanse and clear away our wandering thoughts, keeping them from becoming too strong and the mainstream of our mind. This is what the Consciousness-Only School talks about — instead of using polluted perception to recognize and discriminate phenomena, we use Buddhadharma to observe and investigate the body, mind, and world. We then can use the core teaching of no-self and emptiness to contemplate the original nature of phenomena. No matter what situation appears, follow this core of the noble truth. By continuously doing so, gradually Buddhadharma will become the mainstay of our thinking. Then, when encountering anything, contemplation on emptiness and no-self will enable and assist us to cleanse affliction and eliminate unnecessary impediments. In other words, if you find you have difficulty using the method well, it is fine, and you can try to first cleanse the "pollutant". Slowly you will find yourself able to apply the method.

There Is Only the Method

In early times when I participated in Master Sheng Yen's retreats in Taiwan, he taught us the method of counting the breath, and we all followed his guidance sincerely. In the beginning, there were lots of wandering thoughts, and most of us were unable to count well, but slowly we got better at it. After a while we put down the counting and concentrated on the breathing. When the conditions of stillness and single-mindedness are reached, doubt naturally arose. Shifu (Master Sheng Yen) designed this counting method using seven phases. The first is when wandering thoughts in our mind seem to be endless. The second is when the appearance of wandering thoughts is reduced and breath counting is more continuous. The third is when one is very clearly aware of the counts while there are some wandering thoughts floating over. The fourth feels like no wandering thoughts. The fifth is called "three minds" — the one observing the breath, the counting, and the breath. In the sixth phase, there is only the single-mind. The last phase is "no-mind".

When the body and mind are unified, this is a state of samadhi. When our mind is in such a condition, handling of daily life flows more naturally, as in the saying, "When there is no mind anywhere, it is the time of practicing everywhere." Time and space are one, and it becomes effortless. When you look at the world, you feel nothing has changed but everything is beautiful and intimate, so much so that if one were to accidentally step on a tree leaf while walking, one would feel shy or sorry about it.

In retreat we often see two kinds of expressions on the faces of participants — one is very serious, maybe because they do not do well with the method and are stressed by this, or their personality is usually like this. The second type is happy and jolly. It can be that they are happy even though their mind is in a coarse condition and unable to use the method, or they are just relaxed while using the method. In any case, for practice to be fruitful, particularly in a Chan retreat, one must be sincere and simple-minded in truly applying the method.

I first began learning Chan from Shifu when he was young, around fifty. In leading retreats he was very vigorous and skillful in teaching the students to benefit from the practice of the methods. He was very aware of everyone's condition. Back then, whatever Shifu taught us, we did wholeheartedly. We prostrated when it was time to prostrate, walked when it was time to walk, and everyone was completely engaged in the method. In retreat, the fewer one's opinions, the better one is able to resonate with the method, and the more easily one is able to apply it. The methods are aids to help us break our habits and let go of our self-centered opinions. If you add your own opinion in using the method, you would be following your old habits no matter how you apply the method. Some people participated in many Chan retreats and became "thick skinned investigators". For example, they knew the retreat rules so they looked for imperfections outwardly, and when they could not sit well, they used all sort of tricks to cover it up. Having a beginner's mind is usually less complicated, and one is more able to follow the instructions given by the teacher. With the methods taught systematically, if you follow the instructions step by step, you will be successful. If the retreat were designed to meet the needs of each and every student individually, in the end, everyone would just do their own thing, and it would be impossible to learn the complete system and to wholeheartedly practice. Actually we do what is necessary to accommodate participants in such a way that even if one cannot sit due to physical constraints, one can still hear the teachings of the Dharma.

So, when practicing in the Chan hall, give yourself completely to it by simply using the method. If you cannot wholeheartedly engage in the method and have too much hesitation, it will be impossible to break through attachments to the self. If you focus on the self and keep thinking, "my feet will hurt when I run," or "I will sweat when I run and will have to take a bath," you add clinging to this "I." If you add lots of thinking, it is not easy to apply the method. During the retreat, there are also lots of things to make us comfortable. When your mind is focused on these conditions of comfort instead of being focused on the method, it is difficult to make progress. When we were in retreat in the old days, we did not have peppermint oil or cold medicine readily available. People often took a shower only after a seven-day retreat, and there was no one noticing whose body smelled – we used all our time and energy on the practice of our method. Even when we were so tired and would nod off a few times, we would still continue to practice. Nowadays, the retreat is like a vacation, some people even bring the bath soap they are accustomed to using at home! How could they possibly be letting go of everything and wholeheartedly diving into the method? In a way, the retreat rules are not for restraining anything but rather for reminding you to put effort into practice. Through the disciplined routines we follow with the group, we cleanse and let go of our old habits.

In practice, do not expect particular states to appear or cling to the thought of having reached some state. If you feel you have seen this or realized that, with the "I" and "what I do," or the object and the one who observes the object, this indicates that it is not genuine realization. What are the functions of a Chan retreat? One of them is to test how you have practiced, and another is hopefully to overcome obstacles and experience some sort of breakthrough in a short period of time.

Some people are impatient during walking meditation. When they are instructed to put focus on their own feet, they instead focus on the feet of the person in front of them, often complaining about why that person walks so slowly; or they walk at their own pace or do some kind of alternate step as if showing off as some people do in sitting meditation. If one really uses the method, in slow walking meditation, one should sink the mind to the bottom of the feet with the mind unmoving. This way when you do run fast, you will not feel tired for you can run without feeling your breath and with only the mind of running. In this condition of body and mind unified, the practice of asking the Huatou becomes very useful.

In the Chan hall in early times, those who wholeheartedly dove into practice were able to reach the state of forgetting the self, thus becoming truly single-minded in the method and able to utilize every minute to go deeply. They were able to put down many things without any burden and to just practice. We should really practice like this, without concerning even for the worst, which is death. If one should die in the Chan hall, it is probably unlikely that one will fall into undesirable or evil destinies. Like someone said, "As long as there is the Dharma, what is there to fear?" Since there is right view as guidance, death is not a problem. When one can truly put down the concern about death, practice in retreat can have the power that the experience of breakthrough needs.

Some people, even before the retreat has concluded, are already thinking and planning what to do after they go home. Actually, if you have done well with the method, you will probably be very relaxed and it will be easier to maintain calmness and clarity. As you face whatever you encounter in daily life, your reactions will be more natural and free of unnecessary thinking. Sometimes, however, after being on retreat, you may have residue attachment, such as expecting the state of unification to appear when you do sitting meditation at home. For practitioners in the modern world, with so many trivial affairs in daily life and a lack of self-discipline in studying the Dharma, such expectations create conflict in the mind and are actually counterproductive.

Life after Retreat

Chan Master Ma-Zu Dao-Yi has a famous saying, "Ordinary mind is the Way." This is saying that, all the methods we use in practice start from Buddha-nature. These methods are not only used in sitting meditation, but are constantly in use in our daily activities. We often see masters teaching the disciples during farming. In other words, Chan is in everyday life. Why? Because in every routine activity, one must train oneself to be aware with no-self — with emptiness, Buddha-nature and true suchness. However, it seems that people want to be Buddha only while in retreat. In daily life, they want to be a human being which is much easier than being Buddha because they have too many habits and afflictions. If one does not practice in daily life but only does so in retreat for one or two weeks a year, actually the retreat cannot do much to help you. The strength gained from retreat should be extended to daily life. If one really practices diligently, one finds that the more you practice, the more you are in accord with the Dharma. If one can settle into a deep samadhi state, the realization will be deep and the understanding will be clear. This will help one to adjust habits in daily life.

Even with a busy daily schedule, if you can just sit a little bit each day, it can help you to brush off some of the wandering thoughts and afflictions accumulated through the day. If you can practice like this consistently, the mind condition will be more stable. As benefits from retreat are being extended into daily life, you will not feel practice and daily life to be two separate things. This is the so-called "ordinary mind" which is the mind of practice that can operate in daily life — it does not fluctuate with the turmoil of one's external environment.

Practice ought to follow the middle path. What is the middle path? It is in the proper balance. Often we are unable to follow the middle path — we either over do it or completely fail to use right effort. Balance is needed. How do we find balance? Not by adding something additional but by subtracting or eliminating something from the side that is over. In the end the two sides will definitely be balanced. Why? Because both ends will be empty. Without anything added, it is original stillness and clarity.

Wisdom of Bodhisattva Path

During recent retreats, I have been reading the Great Wisdom Treatises by Nagarjuna (150–250 CE, considered one of the most important Buddhist philosophers after the historical Shakyamuni Buddha). In the works of Nagarjuna, The Middle Treatises is very deep, requiring both philosophical and logical thinking in order to clearly understand what he was saying about the principle of "middle" and "empty". The more I read, the more interesting I find it. In talking about emptiness in the Great Wisdom Treatises, he combines the theory of emptiness with practice and mentions that, in practicing the bodhisattva path, one must perceive emptiness in the wholesome dharma.

The first thirty-two volumes of Great Wisdom Treatises mainly explain many terms in Buddhism, such as the four dhyanas, the four immeasurable minds, and the eight liberations, etc. We usually pay much attention to this section as it is said to be the encyclopedia of Buddhist terms. It includes many religious fairy tales, and it does not merely tell stories but rather exhibits the Dharma and expresses the spirit of the bodhisattva path.

Regarding the bodhisattva path, the Buddha often told stories about his previous lives. For example, in one lifetime he was a king who saw an eagle trying to catch a pigeon. The king wanted to protect the pigeon. The eagle said, "if you protect this pigeon, I will have nothing to eat and I wll die. You care only about the pigeon, and this is not the way of bodhisattvas." The dilemma was that the eagle wanted to eat flesh which necessitated the killing of another animal. The king tried to cut his own flesh to feed the eagle. The eagle said, "Oh, to do so, the weight of the meat has to be the same as that of the pigeon." Let us think, how much does a pigeon weigh? Who knows! Anyway, after the king cut some of his flesh, the weight was still not enough, and he then laid his body on the scale, prepared to feed his entire body to the eagle. At that moment, the eagle and the pigeon showed their original form as great saints who were trying to test the spirit and bodhisattva vows of the king. They asked, "Do you have regret now?" The king answered, "No." They said that if the king did not have regret, his flesh would grow back. Immediately this is what happened.

This story mainly teaches about the equanimity of giving. When facing a dilemma such as this, sacrificing any life would not be good. To solve the problem, one can only give the self. This kind of story exists in both Theravada and Chinese Buddhism and discusses the bodhisattva practice of giving.

The Theravada tradition believes that, before becoming Buddha, bodhisattavas are ordinary people. However, in the Mahayana tradition, there are categories of ordinary and holy in ranks. The bodhisattvas who are in the holy rank can act with emptiness, and the eighth rank can even teach in the form of Buddha. Avolokitesvara Bodhisattva is above the eighth rank and can appear in the form of a Buddha to preach the Dharma. However, in practicing the bodhisattva path, practitioners must follow the wisdom of emptiness. We think that this would be impossible to do, but it indeed can be accomplished with the wisdom of emptiness. There are many of these stories in the Great Wisdom Treatises. In these volumes of treatises, one can feel the compassion of bodhisattvas. In order to fulfill their vows, when they accomplish these acts, they must learn the wisdom of emptiness of the prajna paramittas (offering of wisdom). Even though Nagarjuna continuously taught about emptiness, he was using the analogy to talk about bodhisattva practice. It helps us to realize that emptiness is not something too profound to understand.

We often think there is a state of emptiness and no-self somewhere out there and we seek for it. But it is not out there, it already is. In deepening your practice by contemplating emptiness, let wisdom have the function of transformation in your mind. Then it will be applicable in daily life. If Dharma study becomes only thinking or the Dharma is treated as knowledge or philosophy, it will not have the power of transformation. Understanding of the doctrine of cause and effect as well as that of emptiness can manifest in daily life. We say that the nature of all dharma is empty and with no-self. This is true not only of ourselves but also of everything which we see and interact with. Thus emptiness is not outside of existence, and Chan practice is not finding emptiness out there. Neither is it finding existence first and then establishing emptiness or a state of no-self — it itself is originally empty. This body and its combination of the five elements is itself empty and no-self. Only because of lacking wisdom are we unable to see its true and original face. When we cannot see this, our mind is confused and deluded, and thus we create many afflictions in action. After seeing it clearly, we can act according to the wisdom of Dharma.

Practice is to see the right path. If we can reflect deeply, wisdom will manifest, and it will be reflected in daily life. If we can observe the world and our immediate environment with wisdom and can try our best to perform our necessary tasks or roles accordingly, lots of problems can be reduced or eliminated. For example, when you are a student, just play the role of a student. If you are a mother, be a good mother. The more wisdom one has, the clearer one can see. In some cases, we do not want to face our duty, or sometimes we neglect our roles. In the journey of life, we face many situations like this. It is important that we make sound judgments with wisdom. It can help us to handle awkward situations and to clear out pollutant in our minds. Do not think that only sitting in the Chan hall or sitting at home is practice — we must let the inner strength from the sitting practice extend into daily life — bit by bit.

I feel it is very important to read and reflect deeply on Nagarjuna's Great Wisdom Treatises since practicing the bodhisattva path has to be like this — in daily life. So, we must do the best within what we can do. At the same time, constantly tell ourself to observe everything with the wisdom of emptiness, reflect with the principle of no-self, and solve problems and impediments in mind. If you can do this, you will find the bodhisattva path is well within reach.

Many stories in this text are exaggerated. Why? Because only by being so can they vividly illustrate the bodhisattva spirit. What we need to examine is the spirit behind these stories. What they demonstrate can be accomplished when practitioners reach a certain state of mind in which wisdom is deep. So we should not think of them as fairy tales but see them as reality, knowing one's wisdom can reach such a height. When I was young, it was sometimes hard for me to imagine why the grown-ups did what they did. This was because my age and wisdom had not reached a level at which I was able to comprehend that those stories were real. For example, some legendary stories about charity events were very awe inspiring. "What a miraculous life they had," we would think, "Would we be able to do such deeds?" Maybe we do not dare to imagine we could, but you should know that for some people, these things are very doable. These stories were conveying a message, which is that the nature of being human is good, and this nature is part of Buddha-nature. Do you have it? Yes, you do. So do what you can in study and practice, and let it fully manifest!

As long as you practice wholeheartedly, you will find that the cultivation of mind will naturally manifest in daily life. You need to know how to let it function, find your own strength, and let it manifest. In this way, the bodhisattva path is not that remote and difficult. If you can know this, then practice and life are not two separate things. If Chan in retreats is on one side and life at home is on the other side, dealing with two lives is very tiring. Why? Because one side is simple and easy, and the other side seems too complex. How would you handle it? Actually complex things follow principles. How to recognize the principle and its nature is precisely the wisdom of Chan practice, and it is right here now.

禅

乙未十月初七
太平延柏

55306547R00134

Made in the USA
Lexington, KY
18 September 2016